İnci Bilgin Tekin

Myths of Oppression
Revisited in Cherrie Moraga's and Liz Lochhead's Drama

İnci Bilgin Tekin

MYTHS OF OPPRESSION
Revisited in Cherrie Moraga's and Liz Lochhead's Drama

ibidem-Verlag
Stuttgart

Bibliografische Information der Deutschen Nationalbibliothek
Die Deutsche Nationalbibliothek verzeichnet diese Publikation in der Deutschen Nationalbibliografie; detaillierte bibliografische Daten sind im Internet über http://dnb.d-nb.de abrufbar.

Bibliographic information published by the Deutsche Nationalbibliothek
Die Deutsche Nationalbibliothek lists this publication in the Deutsche Nationalbibliografie; detailed bibliographic data are available in the Internet at http://dnb.d-nb.de.

∞

Gedruckt auf alterungsbeständigem, säurefreien Papier
Printed on acid-free paper

ISBN-13: 978-3-8382-0308-9

© *ibidem*-Verlag
Stuttgart 2012

Alle Rechte vorbehalten

Das Werk einschließlich aller seiner Teile ist urheberrechtlich geschützt. Jede Verwertung außerhalb der engen Grenzen des Urheberrechtsgesetzes ist ohne Zustimmung des Verlages unzulässig und strafbar. Dies gilt insbesondere für Vervielfältigungen, Übersetzungen, Mikroverfilmungen und elektronische Speicherformen sowie die Einspeicherung und Verarbeitung in elektronischen Systemen.

All rights reserved. No part of this publication may be reproduced, stored in or introduced into a retrieval system, or transmitted, in any form, or by any means (electronical, mechanical, photocopying, recording or otherwise) without the prior written permission of the publisher. Any person who does any unauthorized act in relation to this publication may be liable to criminal prosecution and civil claims for damages.

Printed in Germany

To the canonized and noncanonized ...

In memory of my late grandparents, Yıldız and Mustafa Sami Dinçer

Acknowledgements

I am deeply indebted to Prof. Meral Çileli for all the support she gave me at each and every stage of this study. With her sincere belief in this study, her encouragement in times of difficulty, and her guidance, she made it all possible.

I must express my deepest gratitude to Prof. Nursel İçöz for her invaluable contribution to this study. Her recommendations and insights made this a better work.

I would also like to thank Associate Professor Meldan Tanrısal, Assistant ProfessorNurten Birlik and Assistant Professor Nil Korkut for their suggestions.

I also wish to express my gratitude to all my beloved instructors at METU English Literature Programme, Boğaziçi University English Literature and İstanbul University American Literature Departments for collectively making me fascinated with both literatures.

Another heartfelt thanks goes to Professor Aslı Tekinay, Assoc. Professor Özden Sözalan and Assoc. Professor Ünal Norman whose intriguing drama classes inspired me to work on drama.

I would like to thank Prof.Dilek Çalgan, our present Director at Boğaziçi University School of Foreign Languages, for providing us such a distinct atmosphere of study. Many thanks to my dear colleagues at Bogaziçi University Advanced English Unit for their support and encouragement.

The research I conducted at UCSC Center for Cultural Studies has contributed a lot to this study. Many thanks to Professor Chris Connery and Professor Gail Hershatter for accepting me as a visiting scholar and for providing an office, a library access and making me a member of the Friday sessions. I would also like to thank Cherrie Moraga for the interview at Stanford University Theater Arts Department which inspired a big part of the project. Many thanks to Professor Tony Crowley for making me familiar with Liz Lochhead's adaptations.

Many thanks to my dear family, Bülent Tekin, Mert Tekin, Servet Bilgin, Leman Bilgin and Güller Bilgin, for being with me through all this process,tolerating my temper and frequent journeys. Without their enduring emotional support and understanding it would not have been possible.

Table of Contents

1. Introduction 11
   1.1. Methodology 18

2. **A Theoretical Background of Myths and Oppression** 21
   2.1. Myths from a Socio-historical Perspective 21
   2.2. Postcolonialism and Feminism 22
   2.3. Intertextuality and Rewriting 39

3. **Euro-centric Myths and Oppression** 45
   3.1. Signs of Oppression in Euripides' *Medea* 47
   3.2. Sophocles' *The Theban Plays* in Relation to Oppression 53
   3.3. Structures of Oppression and the Aristotelian Tradition 58

4. **Ethnic Roots Retraced** 63
   4.1. A Background on Scottish, Celtic and Aztec, Mayan Myths 64
   4.2. Notes on the Scottish and Chicano/a Traditions of Writing 73
   4.3. Cherrie Moraga and Liz Lochhead's Drama in their National Canons 77

5. **Rewriting Myths of Hierarchical and Colonial Oppression** 87
   5.1. Liz Lochhead's Scottish Patriotism in *Medea* and *Thebans* 87
   5.2. A Postcolonial Perspective to Cherrie L. Moraga's *The Hungry Woman: A Mexican Medea* and *Heart of the Earth: A Popul Vuh Story* 100
   5.3. A Comparative Perspective on Lochhead and Moraga's Representations of Hierarchical and Colonial Oppression 112

6. Revisiting Myths of Gender Oppression 115

  6.1. Lochhead's Mainstream Feminism in *Medea* and *Thebans* 115

  6.2. Moraga's Colored and Lesbian Feminism in H*ungry Woman: A Mexican Medea* and *Heart of the Earth: A Popul Vuh Story* 130

  6.3. A Comparative Approach to Lochhead and Moraga's Feminist Voices and Structures 142

7. Conclusion 147

Works Cited 151

1. Introduction

The purpose of this study is to examine the rewritings of myths of oppression by two contemporary playwrights, Liz Lochhead and Cherrie Moraga, in their authentic contexts, Scottish and Chicana/o respectively, and with their different feminist voices. Thus this study also focuses on the noncanonized Celtic, Scottish and Aztec, Mayan myths which not only form a big portion of Scottish and Chicana traditions of writing but also set the themes and patterns, respectively, of Lochhead's and Moraga's alternative plays.

Drawing on postcolonial and feminist theories, this study claims that in their themes and structures, Western myths involve ethnic, racial, hierarchical and gender oppression. Tracing the recent trends in rewriting the classics to a formally expressed stance against oppression and building on the suggestion made by the Brazilian critic, Augusto Boal, that there is a system of oppression in the Aristotelian tradition, this study compares and contrasts Lochhead's and Moraga's rewritings of these oppressive themes and structures in Western myths.

Western literature derives from Greek mythology. The legends of Olympian gods and goddesses and heroes—born from a deity and a human— might be taken to be representatives of an ancient creed system. From *The Odyssey* and *The Iliad* one can derive the desire of ancient man for a good name and immortality. The intrusion of Athena and Poseidon in Odysseus's journey might be considered representative of the dual forces of nature, controlling man's life. The challenging battle between Hector and Achilles might be considered the survival of the fittest. Both of these stories also imply a search for power and dominance which are among man's basic needs. Major works in various genres of western literature involve themes of oppression through their representations of master versus servant, the superior versus the subordinate; in general, the self versus the other.

Beowulf (700 A.D.), which is considered to be the earliest example of English literature, deals with a fatal struggle between a hero and a monster. Beowulf's fight with Grendel may imply an early pattern of a search for dominance on the other. Major works in different genres of Western literature involve themes of master and servant relations. Cervantes's *Don Quixote* (1604), for instance, introduces the two major characters, Don Quixote and Sancho Panza in such a master and servant relation, respectively. While Don Quixote is depicted as a man of noble blood with chivalric ideals, Sancho Panza is introduced as his subordinate; a common, pragmatic man of lower class. Most plays by William Shakespeare involve similar master and servant relations. Hamlet's attendants, Rosencrantz and Guildenstern, are noteworthy as well as Othello's servant Iago. However Iago sets a different example of servitude through his betrayal of Othello. *Othello* (1604) is a significant play also for its representation of ethnic prejudice against Othello, the Moor. The following lines by Othello exemplify his internalization of his own ethnic Otherness:

> Haply for I am black,
> And have not those soft parts of conversation
> That chamberers have; or for I am declined
> Into the vale of years—yet that's not much— . (l 267-270)

Emily Bronte's *Wuthering Heights* (1847) might be considered among the most noteworthy examples of ethnic prejudices. The following lines in Lockwood's narration imply just such a preconditioning against Heathcliff's ethnic background:

> But Mr. Heathcliff forms a singular contrast to his abode and style of living. He is a dark-skinned gypsy in aspect, in dress and manners a gentleman, that is, as much a gentleman as many a country squire… . (4)

A Passage To India by a contemporary author, E. M. Forster, involves similar patterns of ethnic prejudice which, in turn, suggests that Western literature has been exemplifying such oppression for many centuries. The following quote from the novel exemplifies this sort of preconditioning: "Aziz was exquisitely dressed, from tie-pin to spats, but he had forgotten his back-collar stud, and there you have the Indian all over; inattention to detail, the fundamental slackness that reveals the race" (87).

Ancient Greek writings also involve a repressive attitude towards women, who are represented mostly as secondary characters or even as by-standers. Women hardly play more than an instrumental role in most of these writings. For instance, in *The Odyssey,* Odysseus's wife Penelope, appears only in one of the episodes among many. She is always praised for her patience and loyalty, not as a good person but rather as a good wife. The beauty of Helen of Troy was the reason for the Trojan War. However her personal qualities remained secondary to her beauty, which is a male concern. Similarly, Oedipus's emotions after he learns the truth about his identity is of primary significance and while Jocasta suffers as much, her side of the story is hardly central to the play. Euripides' Medea has always been called the wicked figure of the play while there are no more than a few negative utterances regarding Jason, whose betrayal of Medea is the main source of their tragedy.

Western literature also reflects an oppressive attitude towards women with its stereoypical representations of women. Women are either portrayed as good wives or as good mothers. Unconventional female characters usually lack morality. For instance the depiction of the Wife of Bath in Chaucer's *Canterbury Tales* (written in 1380s) as an independant woman goes parallel to her lack of conventional moral values. When she attends the funeral of one of her husbands, she notes that she can not help thinking about the beauty of his legs, which was quite unconventional in her time. Written many centuries later than the *Canterbury Tales*, Daniel Defoe's *Moll Flanders* (1722), Gustav Flaubert's *Madame Bovary (1857)*, and Margaret Mitchell's *Gone With The Wind* (1936), reflect the same image of a passionate woman who is capable of anything to reach her aim, which involves ignorance of the ethical rules of her time and the victimization of others. The following lines in *Moll Flanders*, uttered by Moll Flanders herself, support this idea:

> The moral indeed of all my History is left to be gather'd by the senses and Judgement of the Reader; I'm not qualified to preach to them, let the Experience of the Creature completely Wicked, and completely Miserable be a Storehouse of useful warning to those that read. (264)

The stereotypical representation of women as good wives and mothers also has a long history. Penelope in Homer's *Odyssey* (written in the late eighth century BC) is possibly one of the earliest representations of a good wife. Shakespeare's *The Taming of The Shrew* (1592*)* is a good example of writing that stages women's position in a patriarchal world. When Petruchio finally manages to "tame" Kate, who used to be a difficult woman, the following lines of the tamed Kate signify internalized patriarchy:

> Thy husband is thy lord, thy life, thy keper,
> Thy head, thy sovereign, one that cares for thee,
> And for thy maintenance commits his body
> To painful labor both by the sea and land,

> To watch the night in storms, the day in cold,
> Whilst thou liest warm at home, secure and safe,
> And craves no other tribute at thy hands
> But love, fair looks, and true obedience-
> Too little payment for so great a debt. (109, 1 162-169)

In the above lines, Kate mentions the major duty of a wife which she calls "true obedience" and notes that this is nothing when the duties of a husband are considered. Her comments below on women exemplify the stereotypical perspective on unconventional women:

> I am ashamed that women are so simple
> To offer for war where they should kneel for peace,
> Or seek for rule, supremacy, and sway
> When they are bound to serve, love and obey. (V.2, 1177-1180)

Unfortunately, there is hardly any change in the situation of women within the subsequent three centuries. The nineteenth-century English (Victorian) novel involves a limited representation of women who are made to fit into a conventional and patriarchal framework. Even the flourishing of governesses does not attribute to women the comfort of being a working woman. Their jobs are already designed to reinforce the territory of women as occupying the domestic sphere. Jane Eyre and Agnes Grey can be recalled among such female characterizations.

In the English canon, Jane Austen's *Pride and Prejudice* and *Sense and Sensibility* and in the American canon, Louisa May Alcott's *Little Women* might be considered among the depiction of women within a patriarchal household. Hence domesticity is another common element in these novels. While mothers are stereotypically interested in their daughters's marriages, daughters attend gatherings to meet rich and handsome candidates. The victimization of women by conventional, patriarchal systems is another common theme in English and American Literature. In Thomas Hardy's *Tess of D'urbervilles* and Nathaniel Hawthorne's *The Scarlet Letter*, the heroines suffer from the prejudices and preconditionings towards unconventional women. The following lines that foreshadow the victimization of Tess also state that Tess, who used to be "So sweet, so good, so true" (316), did not deserve such an end:

> Clare came close, and bent over her. "Dead, dead, dead!"
> he murmured. After fixedly regarding her for some moments
> with the same gaze of unmeasurable woe he bent lower, enclosed
> her in his arms, and rolled her in the sheet as in a shroud. Then

> lifting her from the bed with as much respect, as one would show to a dead body, he carried her across the room, murmuring, "My poor poor Tess, my dearest darling Tess! So sweet, so good, so true." The words of endearment, withheld so severely in his waking hours, were inexpressibly sweet to her forlorn and hungry heart. If it had been to save her weary life she would not, by moving or struggling, have put an end to the position she found herself in. Thus she lay in absolute stillness, scarcely venturing to breathe, and, wondering what he was going to do with her, suffered herself to be borne out upon the landing. "My wife—dead, dead!" he said. (316)

The following quote from *Hamlet* also echoes the preconditioning and prejudice that women in patriarchal cultures are exposed to: "Frailty, thy name is woman" (I.2).

There is hardly any sympathetic depiction of an unconventional female character until the twentieth century. With Virginia Woolf's introspection technique, the inner world of women started to be truly depicted. Doris Lessing's *Marta Quest*, Kate Chopin's *Awakening* may also be considered among the early feminist writings. The contemporary British and American feminist novel introduces many successful women writers such as Jean Rhys, Iris Murdoch, Jeanette Winterson, Angela Carter and Alice Walker, Toni Morison, Ana Castillo. Dramatic representations of striking women characters went parallel to this wave. After Henric Ibsen's *A Doll's House*, the female experience became central to 20th-century drama. In contemporary British and American theatres we find a number of striking women playwrights and their challenging female characters. While the British canon includes Caryl Churchill, Liz Lochhead, Anne Devlin, Sarah Daniels, Pam Gems and Timberlake Wertenbaker ; Marsha Norman, Beth Henley, Wendy Wasserstein, Adrienne Kennedy, Ntozake Shange, Josephina Lopez and Cherrie Moraga are among their American counterparts.

What lies beneath such a challenge to the conventional depictions and representations of women is most certainly the feminist movement which started in the eighteenth century. The goal of early feminists was no more than the attainment of women's human rights. Mary Wollstonecraft and John Stuart Mill may be recalled among the pinoneers of feminism. In the early twentieth Century, women's political rights were also claimed by the Suffragettes. Later, so-called first wave feminism (the nineteeth and the early twentieth centuries) aimed to make women socially equal to men. With the second wave, (1960s and 70s) the focus were shifted toward women's studies, in which women were treated no longer as the 'Other'[1] but as an alternative center. Finally, third wave feminism (1990s to the present) introduces subcategories within feminism such as Marxist-feminism, French feminism, African-American, third-world, and lesbian feminism.

Postcolonialism is another significant movement rising after poststructuralism. Although there are different trends in feminism, as mentioned above, feminism commonly and broadly deals with female oppression in a patriarchal structure:

Its major concern is to reveal the power relations between the West and the East or between "the Occident" and "the Orient" as Edward Saïd calls them (1, 2). When the postcolonial perspective is adapted, all Western values, thoughts and writings are "guilty of a repressive ethnocentrism" since they "have dominated world culture, marginalising or excluding non-Western traditions and forms of cultural life and expression" (Selden and Widdowson 188).

Selden and Widdowson note that not only the methods of deconstruction but also Bakhtin's dialogics, Gramsci's notion of hegemony, Foucault's essays on power and knowledge have inspired postcolonialism (189). Edward Saïd's *Orientalism* (1978), one of the major postcolonialist works, suggests that Western Historicism, which has dominated world history, involves privileged Eurocentricity and that the Orient is a product of Western discourse (3 -28).

Homi Bhabha's notion of "hybridity" as a negotiation of binary opposites and Henri Louis Gates's suggestion of African-American vernacular traditions and oral literature as a structure for black semiotics are among the major contributions to postcolonial thought.

Recently women writers with different ethnic or racial backgrounds have been struggling for their place within the contemporary British and American canons. Among such writers, one can recall Jean Rhys (Creole), Toni Morrison (Black American), Alice Walker (Black American) and Ana Castillo (Chicana). In drama Liz Lochhead (Scottish), Anne Devlin (Irish), Adrienne Kennedy (Black

---

[1] In this study the word Other is used in Simone De Beavoir's conception of women as the Other of man and Edward Saïd's sense of the term as the colonized, in feminist and postcolonial contexts.

American), Ntozake Shange (Black American), Suzi-Lori Parks (Black American), Josephina Lopez (Chicana) and Cherrie Moraga (Chicana) may be the most striking ones.

Feminist and postcolonial resistances go parallel to each other as they share a common ground, namely the oppression of the minor or the 'Other'. Feminist and postcolonial theories and their reflections on contemporary British and American female canons are also central to the scope of this research as these approaches will be used to treat the revisitation of myths by two contemporary women playwrights, namely Liz Lochhead and Cherrie Moraga, both of whom are interested in transcribing their individual and collective experiences with ethnic/ racial and gendered oppression.

Twentieth-century women's writing, especially the writings of women of a minority ethnic or racial background, reflect a change from remembrance to resistance which greatly contributes to British and American writing not only thematically but also in terms of form. This study aims to provide an orientation to Western myths of oppression on the one hand and on the other to a variety of alternative writings in contemporary British and American women's drama. Their recurrent patterns of repetition and resistance to the oppressive myths of patriarchal and colonial Europe are further examined.

A postcolonial-feminist approach is used to treat the plays of the two contemporary women playwrights, Liz Lochhead (Scottish-from the British canon) and Cherrie Moraga (Chicana-from the American canon), which revisit the old Western stories of oppression by integrating their female experiences and (respectively) Scottish and Chicana/o heritages. Postcolonial and feminist studies commonly suggest a thorough liberation of mind and body from the colonial or patriarchal experience. Thus it is the ultimate goal of this study to examine Lochhead's and Moraga's authentic representations of oppression and resistance as well as to discuss, from a comparative perspective, to what extent Lochhead's and Moraga's theatres realise a liberation or 'decolonisation' in the context of fiction writing.

1.1. Methodology

The introductory chapter introduces different perspectives to the understanding of the significance and function of myths. This chapter also suggests an involvement of oppressive power structures in Greek myths and early European writings, with references to British and American canons to which Liz Lochhead and Cherrie Moraga belong. A feminist and postcolonial resistance to this convention is briefly introduced in this chapter as well.

Chapter 2 provides a theoretical background on feminist and postcolonial theories since these theories are essential to understanding the challenges to conventional myths of oppression. This chapter also introduces the theoretical background to rewriting to support later chapters, in which Liz Lochhead's and Cherrie Moraga's rewritings are related to a stance against oppression that expresses itself in dramatic form.

Chapter 3 deals with early Euro-centric myths implying conventional power structures. Euripides' *Medea*, Sophocles' *Oedipus the King, Oedipus at Colonus* and *Antigone* are examined as early examples of oppression in Europe. This chapter also focuses on these plays from the perspective which the Brazilian critic Augusto Boal offers, in relation to the oppression in Aristotelian tradition expressed through its form.

Chapter 4 foregrounds myths of alternative cultures, which, for colonial reasons, have never been centralized. This chapter also explores some Mayan and Aztec as well as Gaelic and Scottish myths in relation to oppression since both Lochhead and Moraga make use of these myths as a challenge to the Eurocentric canon. This chapter also provides an orientation to Lochhead's and Moraga's formally expressed resistance to oppression, relating them to Augusto Boal's conception of "the Theatre of the Oppressed."

Chapter 5 focuses on Moraga's *Hungry Woman: A Mexican Medea* and *Popul Vuh* as well as Lochhead's *Medea* and *Thebans,* as plays rewriting myths of ethnic/racial and hierarchal oppression. This chapter also offers a comparative perspective on Lochhead's and Moraga's individual stances and alternative dramatic techniques, in relation to postcolonial theory.

Chapter 6 deals with Cherrie Moraga's and Liz Lochhead's plays as two striking representatives of feminist rewritings of myths which signify patriarchal oppression. Moraga's *Hungry Woman: A Mexican Medea* and *Popul Vuh* as well as Lochhead's *Medea* and *Thebans* are examined in relation to their distinct and authentic feminist stances and structures.

The conclusion deals with the authenticity in Lochhead's and Moraga's dramatic rewritings in terms of rememberance or/and resistance of/to the conventional themes and structures of oppression. This chapter finally discusses Lochhead's and Moraga's individual social and political stances and techniques in revisiting these myths of oppression.

2. A Theoretical Background of Myths and Oppression

2.1. Myths from a Socio-historical Perspective

Myths can be considered stories which represent early belief systems accounting for the order of the universe. Joseph Campbell defines the function of 'Myths' through a quotation from Shakespeare "to hold, as 't were, the mirror up to nature" (4). He stresses the significance of myths by attributing to them the role of projecting nature. To Edith Hamilton, myths reflect the thoughts and feelings of the human race in told ages. (13) Hamilton also suggests that myths make it possible to "retrace the path from civilized man who lives so far from nature, to man who lived in close companionship with nature; and the real interest of the myths is that they lead us back to a time when the world was young and people had a connection with the earth..." (13). In this respect she views myths as indicators of the collective past of mankind.

Throughout history, mankind has formulated belief and value systems as well as folk traditions which are reflected in legends. The recurrent patterns and elements in such legends in turn formulate the study of myths as mythology. Joseph Campbell argues that myth's functions are, among other things, "to reconcile waking consciousness to the mysteries of this universe" and "to enforce a moral order" (4). He further suggests that by trying to generate a cosmology, an image of the universe, myths also signify the transformation of the image of the universe (611). Drawing upon Campbell's suggestion, myths can be considered both reflectors and reinforcers of patterns leading to an idealized social system.

Different schools view myths from different standpoints. For instance the structuralists take myth as a kind of language, with its system of oppositions. According to the structuralist view, the encoded messages in myths make it possible to introduce a reconciliation to such binary opposites. Freud's psychoanalytical perspective takes myths symbolically, suggesting that they represent the unconscious. Archetypal criticism foregrounds the similarity and repetition of certain patterns and elements in myths of different cultures and traditions. Carl Gustav Jung suggests that myths involve certain repetitive structures which he calls archetypes reflective of mankind's collective unconscious. According to Jung, mankind has a shared, collective unconscious which he inherits from his ancestors' early experience. Claude Levi-Strauss focuses on the presence of the same logical patterns in all myths.

Finally, the poststructuralists claim that myths are dead, focusing on their 'self-deconstruction'. With his definition of myth in *Mythologies,* Roland Barthes gets closer to Terry Eagleton's notion of ideology as he suggests that myth is the notion of a "socially constructed reality" which is introduced as "natural" (74). Barthes notes that the ideas and judgements of a socially specific class are considered "universal truths." He also argues that the real power relations in society (between classes, between coloniser and colonised, between men and women etc.) are obscured, "reference to all tensions and difficulties blocked out, glossed over, their political threat defused " (74-77). Similarly Jacques Derrida suggests:

> The white man takes his own mythology, Indo-European mythology, his own *logos,* that is, the *mythos* of this idiom, for the universal form of that he must still wish to call *Reason* . (7)

The above quote from Derrida implies the canonization and standardization of White mythology, which further signifies the oppression of mythologies considered Other. This suggestion, along with the postcolonial views, is very central to this research as the purpose of this study is to examine the rewriting of myths of oppression by the two contemporary women dramatists (Cherrie Moraga and Liz Lochhead) from a postcolonial feminist perspective. Their rewriting of Greek myths will be analyzed as signs of either remembrance of early European writings or resistance to them.

2.2. Postcolonialism and Feminism

Many theoretical movements emerged in the 20th century, which witnessed many traumatic incidents including the two world wars, the holocaust, the use of atomic weapons, colonial violence, the Vietnam War as well as genocidal activity and the activism of fundamentalist religious identities. On the other hand, concepts like freedom, accountability and transparency have been put on the agenda parallel to the notions of globalization and democratic society.

The conflict between the desire for power and humanistic ideals has both initiated and reinforced the study of oppression. The [20. Merriam-Webster Dictionary defines oppression as "an unjust or cruel exercise of authority or power." The French feminist critic Christine Delphy relates the term "oppression" or "social oppression" to a constraint of "a choice, an explanation, a situation that is political" (197-198). In other words, oppression implies an excessive application of one's power which in turn challenges the liberty of the other.

"Logocentric" views which date back to Plato are often related to "oppression" (Boal 9-11) since they imply the authorization of "one side of the binary poles over the other" (Bhabha 40-43), and in turn announce the centralization of power. Jacques Derrida's notion of "deconstruction" which "destroy[s] the [structuralist] logic of the linguistic sign" (7) is noteworthy in relation to its challenge to "logos" by suggesting that meaning cannot simply be traced to a single binary connection between signifier and "signified," since every "signified" is already a "signifier" in another linguistic system (7). Derrida's above-mentioned challenge to the fixation of meaning may be related to postcolonial theories because any fixation might reinforce binary poles. The dialectics of Self and Other set the basis of both post-colonial and feminist theories, involving the power relations between the Master and the Subordinate, the Major and the Minor; finally with the application of power, the Oppressor and the Oppressed. In her work entitled *Feminist Practice £t Poststructuralist Theory*, Chris Weedon defines feminism as "a politics directed at changing existing power relations between women and men in society. These power relations structure all areas of life, the family, education and welfare, the worlds of work and politics, culture and leisure. They determine who does what and for whom, what we are and what we might become" (1). Her lines assert the idea that feminism deals with arbitrary power relations between the two opposite sexes. Similarly, in *The Idea of Culture*, Terry Eagleton notes that the colonialist encounter is "one of Culture with a culture—of a power which is universal, but thereby worryingly diffuse and unstable, with a state of being which is parochial but secure, at least until Culture gets its well-groomed hands on it" (46). Based on the above lines, one can suggest that post-colonial intention is based on challenging such a power structure of dominance between Culture and culture. In this respect, the feminist and postcolonial theories take parallel paths, as they both resist the oppressive power structures.

Although feminist writings can be traced to the late eighteenth century, feminism starts as a search for women's social and political rights in the early twentieth century. The major concern of the first wave feminists is noted as "women's material disadvantages compared to men" (Selden and Widdowson 207). First wave feminism involves noteworthy writers of the Western canon such as Virginia Woolf and Simone De Beauvoir. For instance, Virginia Woolf, in *A Room of One's Own*—published in 1929—suggests that women are domestically and professionally victimized by men. She uses the metaphor of the looking glass for women's situation as they reflect the desired image of men (31, 32). In the same work, Woolf questions why there is no female counterpart to Shakespeare in the sixteenth century and then argues that if woman is to write fiction, she needs a private sphere (40-48).

The French critic Simone De Beauvoir's writing is considered to be a transition from the First Wave to the Second Wave Feminism. Although her major work *The Second Sex* (1949) shares a common ground with the First Wave, it also involves serious criticism about men's biological, psychological and economic discrimination against women. In her introduction to *The Second Sex*, De Beauvoir asserts that woman is different from man and questions why woman is "the Other" (16-19). In turn she suggests a questioning of the center. She further discusses man's conception of himself as the "One" and women as the "Other" and women's internalization of it which, according to her, gives this situation a mythical layer (16-29).

Second wave feminism involves Betty Friedan's *The Feminine Mystique* (1963) and Shulamith Firestone's *The Dialectic of Sex* (1970) as its forerunners. The central concern of this wave may be summarized as the politics of reproduction. Kate Millett's *Sexual Politics* (1969) and Germaine Greer's *The Female Eunuch* (1970) are noted among the major examples of this trend. The most noteworthy work of the second wave is possibly Elaine Showalter's *A Literature of Their Own* (1977) in which Showalter celebrates the British female canon by tracing it from Brontes to Muriel Spark and Doris Lessing.

There are numerous trends after second-wave feminism such as Marxist-feminism, French Feminism, African-American, third-world and lesbian feminism. French feminist criticism includes Julia Kristeva, Helene Cixous and Luce Irigaray, who focus on language as a patriarchal, conventional system of signs and by deconstructing it, they suggest that the female experience can best be told in women's language, in their terms, in 'ecriture feminine'. The so-called third wave feminism, which involves a postcolonial-feminist perspective, also announces challenging theorists such as bell hooks, Barbara Smith, Gayatri C. Spivak and Gloria Anzaldua. The black American theorist bell hooks suggests that the black women are not truly represented within the white feminism and questions "Ain't I A Woman?." In other words hooks asks why white feminists ignore black women's problems and whether feminism is only for the white woman. While the Indian intellectual Spivak raises a similar question in "Can the Subaltern Speak?" and argues that they cannot, the Chicana theorist Anzaldua calls for a spiritual border crossing to liberate the Mexican Chicanas from the Mexican-American borderline. Her view also announces a celebration of Aztlan (a legendary ancestral home of the Nahua, one of the major cultural communities in Mesoamerica).

Although there are different trends in feminism, as mentioned above, feminism commonly and broadly deals with female oppression in a patriarchal structure:

> We identify the agents of our oppression as men. Male supremacy is the oldest, most basic form of domination. All other forms of exploitation and oppression (racism, capitalism, imperialism, etc.) are extensions of male supremacy: men dominate women, a few men dominate the rest. All power situations throughout history have been male-dominated and male-oriented. Men have controlled all political, physical force. They have used their power to keep women in an inferior position. All men receive economic, sexual and psychological benefits from male supremacy. All men have oppressed women.
> (Redstockings Manifesto, Clause III)

The above lines are quoted from one of the oldest feminist manifestos, which asserts the systematic use of male power to oppress women "throughout history." As the manifesto states, the patriarchal structures have controlled all means of power and women have gradually become the subordinate in this "male-dominated and male-oriented" system. Decades later the feminist theorist Kate Millet similarly views patriarchy as a "power-structured" system that oppresses women by conditioning gender relationships, in *Sexual Politics* (23). Feminist theories focus on the idea that literature has conventionally represented women not as "subjects" but as "objects" as it reflects the notions and values of a male-centered system. Thus Elaine Showalter's work *A Literature of Their Own* and the French feminist call for *ecriture feminine* exemplify the search for a female tradition and form in women's writing. As Lynda Hart notes in her introduction to *Making a Spectacle*, the main objective of introducing a female canon of writing is "to re-present women through their own looking glasses" (3).. Hart further argues that the ongoing feminist search for a new dramatic form is displayed by "canceling and deforming the structures that have held women framed, stilled, embedded, revoking the forms that have misrepresented women and killed them into art" which is made possible "[b]y appropriating certain dramatic conventions and methods, subverting their customary usage and turning the lens of objectivity" (3). Hart's lines foreground a deconstructive attitude toward conventional systems of representing women.

The earliest representations of women as Others or objects of patriarchy, date back to Platonic ages. Theatre historians note that during the fifth Century B.C., women were thoroughly excluded from the practice of theatre due to "Attic morality" (Bieber 9). In its discussion of "goodness," Aristotle's *Poetics* owns an oppressive attitude towards women by calling them "inferior to men" and thus places them, together with the slaves, at the bottom of the hierarchical scale of "goodness" (1, 5-8). As Chapter 1 suggests, Western theatre has directly reflected this dominant male gaze in its stereotypical representation of the submissive figures of women, either as domestic housewives subordinate to their husbands or as evil figures challenging figures of male authority. The feminist drama critic Sue-Ellen Case traces this situation to women's enslavement in the "invisible private sphere" while men have direct access to "public life" (6). According to Case,

> [a]s a result of this suppression of real women, the culture invented its own representation of the gender, and it was this fictional 'Woman' who appeared on stage, in the myths, in the plastic arts, representing the patriarchal values attached to the gender while suppressing the experiences, stories, feelings and fantasies of actual women. (7)

In other words, these male-centered representations together created the myth of "women" which in turn reinforced patriarchy and has gradually become the "Other" of women themselves. Case blames all classics and conventions of theatre for being "allies in the project of suppressing real women and replacing them with masks of patriarchal production" (7). Among myths involving gender oppression, the myth of Demeter and Persephone and the myth of Philomela are noteworthy since they are frequently revisited in different canons of contemporary literature.

Both feminist and postcolonial theories have been influenced by poststructuralist thought in different ways. In "Cultural Feminism versus Poststructuralism: The Identity Crisis in Feminist Theory" Linda Alcoff argues that the concept of woman, which is the central issue of contemporary feminism, is hard to conceive since it is loaded with "overdeterminations of male supremacy" (330). Hence, Alcoff further suggests that for women no longer to be the "contrasting Other" of men, a deconstruction of the very self-definition of feminism is necessary (330-331). In this respect, poststructuralist feminism which is also called the French feminism and led by Helene Cixous, Luce Irigaray and Julia Kristeva, is also involved in the third wave feminism. While the above-mentioned theorists specifically focus on how gender was created within language, third wave feminism broadly deals with the queer theory, transgender politics, anti-racism, women-of-color consciousness and postcolonial theory (as it rejects the binary opposites of gender).

Postmodern understanding also inspired postcolonial theory which challenges existing power structures. As postmodernism deals with "the theme of absent centre" (Selden and Widdowson 178), it reinforces the arbitrariness of power structures. The following lines account for the postmodern experience: "Neither the world nor the self any longer possesses unity, coherence, meaning. They are radically 'decentred'" (Selden and Widdowson 178). In this respect, the decentering of the self implies other possible locations for the 'other' which the postcolonial theory calls for. However according to Selden and Widdowson, postcolonial criticism has also "overlapped with the debates on postmodernism" with its serious concern despite the "more playful and parodic" postmodernism (188).

Postcolonial criticism deals with the study of colonial discourse. Its major interest is based on the power relations between the colonizer and the colonized or more broadly, between the oppressor and the oppressed. As mentioned above, postcolonial theorists commonly view Western thought, canon and tradition as "ethnocentric" or "Eurocentric," suggesting that the colonial/imperial power structure has oppressed the non-Western cultures for centuries long. Studying the oppressive discourse in Western texts which in turn construct the superiority of the colonizer as opposed to the inferiority of the colonized, postcolonialism calls for a new scope on power relations as well as the changing of colonial discourse. Frantz Fanon's *The Wretched of the Earth* (1961) which is a revolutionary text as it views the world of the colonized from the point of view of the colonized, can be considered among the early texts of postcolonialism. Another theorist who inspired postcolonialism is definitely Michel Foucault. Edward Saïd and Homi K. Bhabha have also made significant contributions to postcolonial studies with their works *Orientalism* and *The Location of Culture*, respectively.

Michel Foucault introduced his conception of 'discourse' which later has become one of the keywords on postcolonial studies. He suggests three dimensions for the term 'discourse' in his work entitled *The Archeology of Knowledge* (1972). Foucault adds that he refers to the word firstly as "the general domain of all statements," secondly "sometimes as an individualizable group of statements," and finally, "sometimes as a regulated practice that accounts for a number of statements" (80) From the above suggestions, it can be concluded that Foucault treats the term as a means of connection between different statements. The idea that a systematic connection exists within and in-between statements, reminds one of Foucault's argument that if a systematic knowledge is constructed, it inevitably leads to a construction of power structures. In another work, Foucault defines the relation between power/knowledge as directly based on one another (1980: 27). In his work entitled *Truth and Power* (1994), Foucault states that no one is free to apply his/her power since the reality of this world is that there is power outside us which controls our lives and he adds that even truth is "produced and transmitted under control." (131, 132) One can derive from Foucault's writings that he does not separate truth/power and knowledge/discourse; yet he even views them as incorporative. In his 'Afterword' to Dreyfus and Rabinow's book entitled *Michael Foucault: Beyond Structuralism and Hermeneutics*, Foucault accounts for the reason why he worked on power structures and states that in many societies, the "struggle against the forms of subjection—against the submission of subjectivity" has existed for a long time (213). He further states that "we have to promote new forms of subjectivity through the refusal of this kind of individuality which has been imposed on us for several centuries" (216). Foucault later asserts that when one defines the exercise of power as a mode of action over that of others, "one includes an important element, freedom" (221). Foucault's assumption that "power is everywhere" reflects as Dreyfus and Rabinow suggest, "Foucault opposed the project of tracing all meaning back to the meaning-giving activity of an autonomous, transcendental subject" (xix). In this respect, Foucault's approach to power which is 'outside us,' involves criticism not only of sovereignty but also of many forms of power including discourse, which forms the major link between Foucault's ideas on power, discourse and the current postcolonial theories.

Edward Saïd's publication of his work *Orientalism* in 1978 can be considered a significant step in the orientation of postcolonial theory. Saïd was greatly influenced by Foucault's ideas on power and knowledge as well as his conception of 'discourse'. According to Saïd, the Western canon (the writings of the Occident) involves an oppressive discourse relative to the East (the Orient). In his own words, "[t]he relationship between Occident and Orient is a relationship of power, of domination, of varying degrees of a complex hegemony" (5). To Saïd, the notion of the Orient is produced by the Occident and thus involves the legitimization of Western hegemony (he borrows the term from Antonio Gramsci) and, in turn, Eastern subordination through institutions:

> Without examining Orientalism as a discourse, one can not possibly understand the enormously systematic discipline by which European culture was able to manage—and even produce—the Orient politically, sociologically, militarily, ideologically, scientifically, and imaginatively during the post-Enlightenment period. (Saïd 3)

In this respect, he takes Orientalism as an instrument of Western discourse, which not only involves systems of thought but also their corporate institutions (2,3). He further defines Orientalism as "a Western style for dominating, restructuring, and having authority over the Orient." (3) Saïd also maintains that each and every text about the Orient has been full of stereotypical images of the East from the Western perspective and calls for new texts the authors of which would adopt the perspective of the Orient (20). Saïd also challenges the current structures of Western oppression by suggesting that no discourse is fixed for all times, since it depends on power (100).

Henri Louis Gates can also be considered among the significant postcolonial theorists with his original scope on founding a black semiotics as an alternative to the Eurocentric system of literary criticism. In his work entitled *Figures in Black: Words, Signs, and the "Racial" Self* (1987), Gates applies contemporary literary criticism to the close readings of some black texts. He demonstrates that the current literary theories drawn from Western tradition are not adequate in the reading of African American texts. Hence, Gates suggests the black vernacular tradition of writing as an alternative to the Western tradition. In *Signifying Monkey: A Theory of Afro-American Literary Criticism* (1988), Gates traces the roots of African American vernacular tradition of "signifying" which involves double-speech and trickery (xxi) and is used by a character of black vernacular tradition, namely the signifying monkey. Gates uses it in his close reading of some texts by black authors and observes its function as an intertextual reference within the African American literary tradition.

Homi K. Bhabha is another noteworthy postcolonial theorist who in his work *The Location of Culture* (1994), challenges the Western production and implementation of certain binary oppositions such as center versus margin, civilized versus savage, enlightened versus ignorant. Bhabha suggests a destabilization of binary opposites for the cultures to freely interact and even transform one another. Bhabha calls for a reinterpretation of political discourse as a solution to colonization. "Hybridity" and "linguistic multivocality" are among the significant concepts Bhabha views as alternatives to the dislocation of the existing discourse. Another significant concept Homi Bhabha introduces to postcolonial studies is "ambivalence". Bhabha states the function of "ambivalence" in his article entitled "The Other Question" as:

> It is not possible [...] without the attribution of ambivalence to relations of power/knowledge, to calculate the traumatic return of the oppressed—those terrifying stereotypes of savagery, cannibalism, lust and anarchy which are the signal points of identification and alienation, scenes of fear and desire, in colonial texts. (43)

Bhabha contributes to the postcolonial studies especially by foregrounding the in-between, hybrid or ambivalent as a challenge to the privileged side of the binary oppositions.

Feminist and postcolonial studies in common focus on the existing power relations which in turn determine the 'discourse'. The whole system with all its institutions is organized to work for the colonizer and thus needs a revision. The relations between the oppressor and the oppressed have been the common ground of postcolonial and feminist studies. This study draws upon the postcolonial and feminist theories in its conception of ethnic, racial and gender oppression.

Similar to postcolonialism, postfeminism also calls for a new system, involving a new language, to better represent the 'Other'. The postcolonial or third wave feminists deal with both gender and ethnic oppressions. Among them, one can recall bell hooks, Barbara Smith, Gayatri C. Spivak, and Gloria Anzaldua. In this study bell hooks, Spivak and Anzaldua will be focused on since their feminisms involve deconstruction as well.

bell hooks is a black American theorist who contributed a lot to "Third World Feminism" with her question, "Ain't I A Woman?" in her book entitled *Ain't I A Woman: Black Women and Feminism.* There hooks states that white feminism fails to account for the black women's experience. To hooks, black women are exposed to dual oppression as the least priviliged, within the hiearchal scale of white man, white woman, black man and black woman in terms of both race and gender.

> The enslaved black woman could not look to any group of men, white or black, to protect her against sexual exploitation. Often in desperation, slave women attempted to enlist the aid of white mistresses, but these attempts usually failed. Some mistresses responded to the distress of female slaves by persecuting and tormenting them. Others encouraged the use of black women as sex objects because it allowed them respite from unwanted sexual advances. In rare cases, white mistresses who were reluctant to see sons marry and leave home purchased black maids to be sexual playmates for them. Those white women whó deplored the sexual exploitation of slave women were usually reluctant to involve themselves with a slave's plight for fear of jeopardizing their own position in the domestic household. Most white women regarded black women who were the objects of their husband's sexual assaults with hostility and rage. Having been taught by religious teachings that women were inherently sexual temptresses, mistresses often believed that the enslaved black woman was the culprit and their husbands the innocent victims. (36)

In this respect, hooks makes a call for a union within feminist thought. In *Talking Black: Thinking Feminist Thinking Black,* she further suggests that 'oppression' must be considered the leading factor behind both patriarchal and racist discourses. The following lines by her also assign to feminism the role of resisting all systems of oppression:

> Feminism as a liberation struggle, must exist apart from and as part of the larger struggle to eradicate domination in all its forms. We must understand that patriarchal domination shares

> an ideological foundation with racism and other forms of group oppression, that there is no hope that it can be eradicated while these systems remain intact. This knowledge should consistently inform the direction of feminist theory. (22)

Another black feminist theorist, Barbara Smith, agrees with hooks in her approach to white women. In "Racism and Women's Studies" Smith also asks white women to collaborate against all types of oppression:

> White women don't work on racism to do a favor for someone else, solely to benefit Third World women. You have to comprehend how racism distorts and lessens your own lives as white women—that racism affects your chances for survival, too, and that it is very definitely your issue. Until you understand this, no fundamental change will come about. (26)

The above lines by Smith also imply that domination works as a chain reaction, which hence can only be challenged by a systematic stance taken by all women against any means of oppression.

Black feminism, which is the first sub-movement within feminism, unites forces with Other women, involving Asian, Indian, Arab, American Indian, Latina and Chicana women or in short third-world women. They together announce themselves to be women of color and all challenge eurocentrism within feminism.

Gayatri C. Spivak and Gloria Anzaldua are noteworthy among women of color theorists for their original conceptions of "subaltern" and "bordercrossing" respectively. Both Spivak and Anzaldua suggest a deconstruction of the patriarchal and colonial discourses—one through letting the subaltern speak, the other through a spiritual border crossing between dual identities.

Gayatri C. Spivak (1942-) is an Indian author, literary critic and scholar who is currently teaching at Columbia University. Dr. Spivak is well-known for her article entitled "Can the Subaltern Speak?" (she borrows the term from Gramsci), in which she criticizes the power structures for silencing the Other and questions who speaks for whom. In this work, Spivak also examines the Western discourses which in turn speak of/for the 'subaltern' woman (271). In an analysis of Spivak's "Can the Subaltern Speak," Selden and Widdowson argue that "the oppressed and silenced cannot, by definition, speak or achieve self-legitimation without ceasing to be that named subject under neo-colonialism. But if the oppressed subalterns cannot be spoken for by Western intellectuals—because this would not alter the most important fact of their position—nor speak for themselves, there can apparently be no non- or anti-colonial discourse" (194, 195). However, Selden and Widdowson view Western canon's speaking for the 'subaltern' as a significant and necessary step for anti-colonialism. But, Spivak herself is not so optimistic about the subaltern woman being given a voice as she suggests, within the existing structure and institutions. She claims, " the subaltern woman will be as mute as ever" and goes on as follows.

> In seeking to learn to speak to (rather listen to or speak for) the historically muted subject of the subaltern woman, the postcolonial intellectual systematically unlearns female privilege. This systematic unlearning involves learning to critique postcolonial discourse with the best tools it can provide and not simply substituting the lost figure of the colonized. (295)

Spivak's writings have contributed to both feminist and postcolonial theories. Among her other celebrated works, one can consider her translation of Derrida's *Of Grammatology* (1976), *In Other Worlds: Essays in Cultural Politics* (1987), *Selected Subaltern Studies* (edited with Ranajit Guha in 1988), *The Post-Colonial Critic* (1990), *Outside in the Teaching Machine* (1993), *The Spivak Reader* (1995), *A Critique of Postcolonial Reason: Towards a History of the Vanishing Present* (1999), *Death of a Discipline* (2003), and *Other Asias* (2007).

Raman Selden and Peter Widdowson note that "Spivak's work is of special interest because she has made the unsynchronised and contradictory factors of ethnicity, class and gender that compose such identities her own 'subject,'" adding that Spivak "traces this 'predicament of the postcolonial intellectual' in a neo-colonised world in her own case as well as in the texts of the Western or Indian traditions she examines" (194). As Selden and Widdowson also note, Spivak's studies are fed by her personal experience as a 'bilingual' with double identities as an American citizen and an Indian background. In Alfred Arteaga's interview, Spivak accounts for her individual experience as, "I have two faces. I am not in exile. I am not a migrant. I am a green-card-carrying critic of neocolonialism in the United States" (1996: 18). To Selden and Widdowson, the common perspective in Spivak's writing is "the strategy of 'negotiating with the structures of violence' imposed by Western liberalism: to intervene, to question and change the system from within" (194). In this respect, Selden and Widdowson view Spivak as a significant critique of neo-colonialism not only because she speaks for the Other subject and her textuality but also because she challenges the oppressive power structures, not from outside the system but from within. As an Indian scholar teaching at high-ranking institutions in the United States, Spivak struggles with Euroamerican centrism within the American education system as well, viewing it as a "further luxury of 'First World' domination," in Selden and Widdowson's terms (194).

Another significant feature of Spivak's understanding is her Derridian sense of deconstruction which involves both repetition and negation. The following lines, quoted from Spivak's translation of Derrida's *Of Grammatology*, imply these two aspects of deconstruction:

> Operating necessarily from the inside, borrowing all the strategic and economic resources of subversion from the old structure, borrowing them structurally, that is to say, without being able to isolate their elements and atoms, the enterprise of deconstruction always in a certain way falls prey to its own work. (24)

In Alfred Arteaga's interview, Spivak further accounts for her conception of 'deconstruction' as follows:

> Deconstruction does not say there is no subject, there is no truth, There is no history. It simply questions the privileging of identity so that someone is believed to have the truth. It is not the exposure of error. It is constantly and persistently looking into how truths are produced. (1996: 27-28)

In this respect Spivak's understanding of deconstruction goes parallel to Spivak's conception of 'postcolonialism' since she views both as a study of power relations. According to Spivak, in careless hands postcolonialism always has a tendency to become neo-colonialism as the postcolonialists unintentionally recentralize the privileged position. Neocolonialism implies a form of economic imperialism in a contemporary sense, that powerful nations behave like colonial powers forms a similarity to colonialism, in a post-colonial world. After the process of decolonization, the term neocolonialism was introduced to suggest that there is a new form of colonialism, because of the former colonial powers and other developed nations.

Gayatri Spivak suggests, "when a narrative is constructed, something is left out. When an end is defined, other ends are rejected, and one might not know what those other ends are" (1990: 9). Her lines above imply that textuality involves a specific discourse by making choices between possible centers. This idea accounts for Spivak's interest in the representation of the female subject in Western literature " not only as individual but also as 'individualist'" (1999: 116). in Norma Alarcon's words the 'modal person' (Calderon and Salvidar 29).

Gloria E. Anzaldua (1942-2004) is a Mexican American (Chicana) feminist theorist and author who also has an academic background. Anzaldua had taught at San Francisco State University, the University of California at Santa Cruz and Florida Atlantic University and had been working on her PhD dissertation before her death. She contributed not only to postcolonial and feminist theories but also to queer theory. Among Anzaldua's well-known works, one can recall her writing *Borderlands/La Frontera: The New Mestiza* (1987), coediting *This Bridge Called My Back: Writings by Radical Women of Color* with Cherrie Moraga (1981), editing *Making Face, Making Soul/Haciendo Caras: Creative and Critical Perspectives by Women of Color* (1990) as well as her coediting *this bridge we call home: radical visions for transformation* (2002).

Anzaldua's 'This Bridge' series makes a call to Chicana feminists for not being obsessed with hegemonies that situate the white over the colored, the male over the female and even the heterosexual over the queer. In this respect, both works are critical of white textuality which is fed by and in turn continuously reinforces such hegemonies:

> Twenty-one years ago we struggled with the recognition of difference within the context of communality. Today we grapple with the recognition of commonality within the context of difference. While *This Bridge Called My Back* displaced whiteness, *this bridge we call home* carries this displacement further. It questions the terms white and women of color by showing that whiteness may not be applied to all whites, as some possess women-of-color consciousness, just as some women of color bear white consciousness. (2)

The lines quoted above are taken from Anzaldua and Keating's preface to *this bridge we call home: radical visions for transformation*. This work may be considered a celebration of difference while it also aims at raising the consciousness of women of color. Thus Anzaldua and Moraga set their reasons for initiating the project which they view as an "attempt to bridge the contradictions" in their individual experiences:

> We are the colored in a white feminist movement.
> We are the feminists among the people of our culture.
> We are often the lesbians among the straight.
> We do this bridging by naming ourselves and by telling
> our stories in our own words. (23)

The above lines, taken from *This Bridge Called My Back: Writings by Radical Women of Color*, imply resistance to the white world as well as self-recognition among the women of color. The word "bridge is used here as a metaphor for the reconciliation of different identities which are all located by the dominant ideologies on the Other side of the binary pole. In her introduction to *Haciendo caras, una entrada*, Anzaldua distinguishes between white feminism and women-of-color feminism by stating that white feminists try to ignore racial differences by foregrounding that all women and/or lesbians are exposed to sexual/gender oppressions (xxi). She further argues that by foregrounding similarities, the white feminists end up creating Other differences which in turn "widen the gap between white and the colored" (xxi). Moraga and Anzaldua assert in their edition of *This Bridge Called My Back*:

> As Third World women we clearly have a different relationship
> to feminism than the white women but all of us are born into an
> environment where racism exists. Racism affects all of our lives,
> but it is only white women who can 'afford' to remain oblivious
> to these effects. The rest of us have had it breathing or bleeding
> down our necks. (62)

Anzaldua's publication of her book entitled *Borderlands: La Frontera-The New Mestiza* in 1987 brought a different scope to Chicana feminism. There Anzaldua views the *mestizos* as hybrid people, at the crossroads between two different nations, languages and identities. The following lines are quoted from her Preface to the first edition of *Borderlands*:

> I am a border woman. I grew up between two cultures, the
> Mexican (with a heavy Indian influence) and the Anglo (as a number
> of colonized people in our territory). I have been straddling that *tejas*-
> Mexican border, and others, all my life. It's not a comfortable territory
> to live in, this place of contradictions. Hatred, anger and exploitation
> are the prominent features of this landscape.
>
> However, there have been compensations for this *mestiza*, and
> certain joys. Living on borders and in margins, keeping intact one's
> shifting and multiple identity and integrity, is like trying to swim in

> a new element, an "alien" element. There is an exhilaration in being a participant in the further evolution of humankind, in being "worked" on. I have the sense that certain "faculties"—not just in me, but in every border resident, colored or non-colored—and dormant areas of consciousness are being activated, awakened. Strange, huh? And yes, the "alien" element has become familiar—never comfortable, not with society's clamor to uphold the old, to rejoin the flock, to go with the herd. No, not comfortable but home. (19)

In her continuing lines, Anzaldua states that her intention in writing this book is to speak of her existence as well as "to communicate, to speak, to write about life on the borders, life in shadows" (19).

In Anzaldua's conception, the *mestiza* is not only native to the Americas but also the non-Western Other; living on the border which she defines as "a dividing line, narrow strip along a steep edge" (25). Anzaldua also notes that borders determine 'the safe' and 'unsafe places', "to distinguish us from them" (25). To Anzaldua, a borderland signifies a constant state of transition with its prohibited and forbidden inhabitants (25).

Her recognition of her own in-between state as a 'border resident' offers possibilities for what the Chicana theorists call "spiritual bordercrossing," a means of reconciliation between these different identities. Anzaldua claims the mythical homeland of the Aztecs, *Aztlan,* for Chicanas, suggesting that it was their original land before the Gringos appeared: "My grandmother lost all her cattle, they stole her land." (30)

While she calls for a New Mestiza consciousness, she traces the ancestral Aztec roots of the Chicana. The following quote from her poem, published in *Borderlands*, accounts for the inability of Chicanas to encounter and enjoy one side of their identities:

> She has this fear that she has no names that she has many names that she doesn't know her names She has this fear that she's an image that comes and goes clearing and darkening the fear that she's the dreamwork inside someone else's skull. (65)

In the new understanding introduced by Anzaldua, *Aztlan* also serves as a transition between two opposite sides of the binary pole in terms of both ethnicity and gender. In Karin Ikas's interview with her (published in *Borderlands*), Anzaldua accounts for her existence as 'spiritual *mestizaje*' and her philosophy as "a philosophical *mestizaje* where I take from all different cultures for instance, from the cultures of Latin America, the people of color and also the Europeans" (238-239).

Calling for a 'New Mestiza consciousess' which involves a national and ethnic recognition, Anzaldua challenges the dualities of sexuality as well. While she defines the forbidden inhabitants of the borderland as "los atravesados," she names the queer among them. She further explains *los atravesados* as "those who cross over, pass over, or go through the confines of the 'normal'" (25). In this respect, it may be suggested that Anzaldua challenges the conception of 'norm' which favours one side of the binary pole over the other and situates the in-between as the 'abnormal.' Her announcement of herself as both male and female as well as the intergeneric form she uses in *Borderlands* contributes to her focus on the in-between or the hybrid. Doing this, Gloria Anzaldua also introduces a deconstructive perspective to the conventional understanding of the irreconcilable binary opposites.

Gayatri C. Spivak and Gloria Anzaldua have both traced some classical stories involving oppressive discourses and offered possibilities of decentralizing them. In "Three Women's Texts and A Critique of Imperialism" Spivak studies three Western novels, *Jane Eyre*, *Wide Sargasso Sea* (a rewriting of Bronte's *Jane Eyre* by Jean Rhys, from a postcolonial perspective) and *Frankenstein*, from the standpoint of 'self' and 'Other'. There she views Jean Rhys's Creole heroine Antoinette Bertha Mason's story as the unwritten narrative of Bronte's *Jane Eyre*. As Gayatri Spivak suggests, "when a narrative is constructed, something is left out. When an end is defined, other ends are rejected, and one might not know what those other ends are" (1990:9). This argument by Spivak also asks those who read Jean Rys to reread her work, which Spivak accuses of making Antoinette internalize her *self* as her Other. In this respect, according to Spivak, Rhys ends up falling in the trap of most postcolonial writers: While Rhys intends to rewrite *Jane Eyre* from a postcolonial perspective, she can not help involving 'neo-colonial' viewpoints. Focusing on such gaps and delays in Rhys's narrative, Spivak announces that a second rewriting is possible.

In her experimental work entitled *Borderlands: La Frontera*, Gloria Anzaldua rewrites the stories of "*Malinali*," "*la Llorona*" and "*the Virgen de Guadalupe.*" Anzaldua's intention in rewriting these stories may be to centralize the female ancestry of Mexico historically so that she can cross the border spiritually. The following lines, quoted from *Borderlands,* assert that she views Mexican Indian woman as a significant part of her identity: "My Chicana identity is grounded in the Indian woman's history of resistance" (43). In her introduction to the second edition of *The Borderlands*, Sonia Salvidar-Hull suggests that Anzaldua's task there is "to uncover the names and powers of female deities whose identities have been submerged in the Mexican memory of these three mothers. The New Mestiza narrates the pre-Cortesian history of these deities, and shows how they were devalued by both the Azteca-Mexica patriarchs and by the Christian conquerors" (6). Salvidar-Hull also argues that Anzaldua traces the Aztec tradition of migration; thus Anzaldua's Chicana/mestiza feminist experiences a "constantly shifting identity formation" (7).

In their revisitations of these classical stories, both Spivak and Anzaldua challenge not only the representations of conventional systems of oppression but also the discourses through which stories are narrated. In this respect, their foregrounding of a postcolonial-feminist perspective also involves deconstruction as an instrument for possible future reconciliations. Furthermore both their academic backgrounds and individual experiences, what they call the in-between, deeply contribute to their theoretical perspectives. Their studies make a call to female writers with different ethnic origins; encouraging them to retell the old stories, reconstruct alternative histories and re-experience their dual identities by rewriting texts of oppression.

2.3. Intertextuality and Rewriting

In *The Rustle of Language*, Roland Barthes views the text not simply as a gathering of words, implying a "single, 'theological' meaning," but rather as "a multidimensional space" (53). According to Barthes,

> the text is a fabric of quotations, resulting from a thousand sources of culture. [...T]he writer can only imitate an ever anterior, never original gesture, his sole power is to mingle writings, to counter some by others [...] and this book itself is but a tissue of signs, endless imitation, infinitely postponed. (53)

The above quote indicates that a structuralist perspective as a systematic relation of signs is taken as granted while an outside context is assumed as a ground for everlasting references. The same quote also suggests that it is almost impossible to write an original text since the text will inevitably refer to other texts in the "multidimensional space" of all written texts.

In his work entitled *The Reading Process*, Wolfgang Iser also denies the possibility of a finished text:

> Even in the simplest story there is bound to be some kind of blockage, if only for the fact that no tale can ever be told in its entirety. Indeed, it is only through inevitable omissions that a story will gain its dynamism. Thus whenever the flow is interrupted and we are led off in unexpected directions, the opportunity is given to us to bring into play our own faculty for establishing connections—for filling in the gaps left by the text itself. (216)

Iser's assumption, which is central to reader-response theory, implies that when a text is written, it is inevitably written with its gaps, lacks and delays. These gaps and delays enable the reader to go through his or her subjective reading process which attributes to the story an interactive relation with its reader. This is what Iser calls the story's dynamism.

Barthes's later work, especially *The Death of the Author*, involves a poststructuralist approach toward the text, as he gets closer to reader-response criticism. Roland Barthes's distinction between "readerly" and "writerly" texts in his work entitled *S/Z* (4) also supports the idea that both reading and writing will ideally lead to interactive and ongoing processes. Barthes's later work is influenced by the French theorist Jacques Derrida's conception of "deconstruction," which challenges Barthes's former systematic understanding of the sign system. To Derrida, language involves "a play of difference" that is inevitably "permitted by the lack or absence of a center or origin" or of a "transcendental signified" (289).

In this respect, both structuralist and poststructuralist theories view any text as unfinished. Postmodernists focus on the idea that a text may be endlessly rewritten from many different perspectives, celebrating the multiplicity of truth. Although rewriting may imply a possible deconstruction of an already written text, it may also be linked to a reconstruction of an already written text by filling in its gaps and delays from a specific perspective.

In *Of Grammatology*, Derrida further suggests "there is nothing outside of the text" (158), which implies that all texts inevitably refer to themselves. The idea that any text refers to its own textuality connotes the postmodern notion of self-referentiality or metatextuality. The concepts of metatext and metafiction involve a postmodern understanding of the text in which "the text reflects its own status as fictional" (Castle 316). In *Narcissistic Narrative*, Linda Hutcheon traces metafictional devices not only to narcissism but also to "revolutionary activity," in an attempt to "present the unpresentable" (154, 155). Intertextuality can be defined as "[a] theory of textual reference which holds that the relationship between texts within and between DISCURSIVE FORMATIONS is partly determined by citations and allusions" (Castle 315). Julia Kristeva's semiotic approach in *Desire* introduces the term "intertextuality," tracing the Bakhtinian terms "dialogism" and "carnivalesque" to an understanding of writing as "both subjectivity and communication" (68).

Intertextuality inevitably implies the presence of other postmodern devices such as play, parody, pastiche and citation. Gregory Castle considers the postmodern understanding of citation as "a strategy of repetition and appropriation; texts cite each other not with the intent of invoking an authority or showing indebtedness but with the desire to create new expressive connections, new opportunities for enunciation and articulation, new models of cultural production and social action" (146). To Linda Hutcheon, as a postmodern device, postmodern parody may be defined as "ironic quotation, pastiche, appropriation, or intertextuality" (93), Hutcheon suggests that postmodern parody does not intend to neglect the past representations but views them not "nostalgic[ally]" but "critical[ly] and "iron[ically]" (93), celebrating "both continuity and difference" (93), in order to assert that "we are inevitably separated from the past" (94). In this she builds on Fredric Jameson's definition of pastiche.

> Pastiche is, like parody, the imitation of a peculiar or unique, idiosyncratic style, the wearing of a linguistic mask, speech in a dead language. But it is a neutral practice of such mimicry, without any of parody's ulterior motives, amputated of the satiric impulse, devoid of laughter and of any conviction that alongside the abnormal tongue you have momentarily borrowed, some healthy linguistic normality still exists. Pastiche is thus blank parody, a statue with blind eyeballs [;] (Jameson 18) 18)

Castle treats pastiche not as "blank parody" as Jameson does, but rather as a form of intertextuality in which any means of outside reference is alternated by the self-referentiality of a "linguistic universe" (147). Castle's approach then relates intertextuality to self-referentiality, similarly to Linda Hutcheon who, in *A Theory of Parody: The Teachings of Twentieth-Century Art Forms*, considers intertextuality to be a form of "metadiscursive" and "self-reflexive" critique (95, 101).

In this respect the postmodern understanding of the text introduces an inevitable collaboration of intertextuality and self-referentiality, both of which are embodied in the idea of a metatext. When rewriting is considered, both intertextuality and self-referentiality are incorporated in rewriting since rewriting involves an intentional dialogue with another text, the awareness of which also requires an ontological consciousness of its own textuality. Thus any rewriting of any text may be viewed as a metatext which employs one or several of the postmodern devices mentioned above. As a subversive strategy, rewriting implies a deconstruction of the text it rewrites while it also introduces a reconstruction of the same text with a new discourse. In this respect Linda Hutcheon's following lines on postmodern parody are quite applicable to this kind of rewriting: "both deconstructively critical and constructively creative..." (98) and "doubly coded in political terms: it both legitimizes and subverts that which it parodies" (101).

Since rewriting is an effective technique to convey a certain discourse, it has been widely used in contemporary writing. Especially the postcolonialists and feminists who challenge the centralization of one of the binary poles, have a growing interest in rewriting classical texts. Rewriting involves a close dialogue with another work which is quite reminiscent of intertextuality. However, intertextuality, "typically," does not involve "intentionality" in reference (Castle 315) and rewriting implies more than arbitrary intertextual references as it requires a certain objective and/or discourse.

Western myths, which have formed not only the mainstream canon but also the universal standards of literature, involve social and political oppression, as suggested in Chapters 2 and 3. On the other hand, as discussed above, there is a significant interest in postcolonial and feminist theories which commonly suggest a questioning of existing power structures as well as a reconstructon of ethnic, racial and gender codes and signifiers. Many writers in contemporary British and American literatures have been challenging the Euro-centric and patriarchal discourses in Western myths. There is a growing tendency in all canons of literature for rewriting myths, especially those which involve racial/ethnic and gender oppression. Among myths involving oppression, the myths of Demeter and Persephone, Philomela and Apollo-Marsyas, the oppressive structures of which will be examined in Chapter 3, are noteworthy since they are frequently revisited by contemporary writers dealing with oppression. The former two might be considered a great tool for feminist rewriting while the latter two are frequently rewritten in a postcolonial context.

Many writers in contemporary world literature have recently been challenging the dominant patriarchal discourses embedded in Western myths. Especially the female canons of contemporary British and American literature are quite rich in rewriting myths in a postcolonial and/or feminist context. The novel may be considered the most popular genre in such rewriting as it hosts a narrative voice and one or more focalizers which together enable the author to convey his/her message more directly.

The growing interest in rewriting myths from a feminist perspective is also reflected in various genres of British and American literatures. Iris Murdoch, Jean Rhys, Jeanette Winterson, Angela Carter, Alice Walker, Toni Morrison and Charlotte Perkins Gilman are some of the most striking women writers who make use of myths in their feminist fictions.

Contemporary British and American theaters both host feminist rewritings of patriarchal myths. As theatre is a performative art, the critical terms adaptation and transformation mean rewriting in terms of staging. Hence in drama rewriting indicates a textual reconstruction of a play while the terms adaptation and transformation usually refer to a play whose form places it in a new context. Contemporary British and American drama, especially in the female canon, deal with themes of gender and/or racial/ethnic oppression. In the UK Caryl Churchill, Pam Gems, Timberlake Wertenbaker, Winsome Pinnock, Liz Lochhead; and in the US Marsha Norman, Wendy Wasserstein, Beth Henley, Ntozake Shange, Adrienne Kennedy, Josefina Lopez, and Cherrie Moraga are among such noteworthy women playwrights of British and American drama respectively. As discussed above, the rise of postcolonial and feminist studies has introduced a new focus in drama on rewriting myths of oppression. Both British and American drama represent the ethnic/racial and/or engendered Other in challenging contexts by re-presenting their different and old stories.

As discussed above, postcolonial and feminist canons are rich in rewriting myths of oppression rewritten from a deconstructive perspective. Especially ethnic and indigenous groups in Britain and the States have a growing interest in rewriting myths from a postcolonial perspective. The Scottish playwright Liz Lochhead and the Chicana playwright and theorist Cherrie Moraga have both revisited myths of oppression by bringing their own ethnic/racial and engendered contexts into their authentic versions. Their postcolonial and feminist stances in rewriting Western myths of oppression imply both a repetitive and resistant attitude toward these myths. In this respect, Lochhead's and Moraga's attitudes in their rewritings of myths are quite reminiscent of the following lines by Adrienne Rich: "We need to know the writing of the past, and know it differently than we have ever known it; not to pass on a tradition but to break its hold over us" (35).

3. Euro-centric Myths and Oppression

Joseph Campbell defines the function of 'Myths' through a quotation from Shakespeare "to hold, as 't were, the mirror up to nature" (4). Similarly Edith Hamilton notes that "myths reflect the thoughts and feelings of the human race." (13). Both suggestions quoted above attribute to myths the role of reflection. In other words, myths reflect life itself. Considering Western myths, one can realize the oppressive power structures of those times' Europe in terms of class, gender and ethnicity. The origin of Western mythology is Greek and Roman myths and legends in which there is a hierarchy among gods and goddesses, heroes and ordinary men. The twelve great Olympians of Greek mythology that make up a divine family which all have their Roman counterparts as mentioned in parantheses, are listed below according to hierarchy: Zeus (Jupiter) the chief, followed by his two brothers Poseidon (Neptune) and Hades (Pluto), his sister Hestia (Vesta), his wife Hera (Juno), his son Ares (Mars), and his other children; namely Athena (Minerva), Apollo, Aphrodite (Venus), Hermes (Mercury), Artemis (Diana) and finally Hera's son Hephaestus (Vulcan) who only in some sources is considered as Zeus's son, too. The two gods of earth, the corn goddess Demeter (Ceres) and the wine god Dionysus (Bacchus) follow the Olympians in rank.

This structure involves not only a class-based system but also a patriarchal one since all gods and goddesses are classified and defined in their relation to the male chief god, Zeus. In *The Iliad*, Zeus asserts his privileged position among the gods and goddesses as he challenges them at the beginning of Book 8: "I am mightiest of all. Make trial that you may know. Fasten a rope of gold to heaven and lay hold, every god and goddess. You could not drag down Zeus. But if I wished to drag you down, I would" (118). The same hierarchy holds for gods and heroes, heroes and ordinary men. For instance, Odysseus who is praised many times in both *The Odyssey* and *The Iliad* as "godlike," is condemned and punished by Poseidon in *The Odyssey* to a series of long journeys before he reaches his native land (78). In this respect, the status of the hero who is the child of an immortal and a mortal, might be likened to that of the hybrid. In other words, as the in-between, the hero is given the mid-status in such a caste-like classification of nobility.

Early Western myths also imply a patriarchal structure in their approach to women since women are foregrounded only as good mothers who bring up brave warriors. For instance Odysseus's wife Penelope is praised for being a good mother to her son Telemachus and a loyal wife to Odysseus. In the following lines (A. Cook's translation), Penelope asserts her loyalty, even years after Odysseus's departure.

> So I pay no heed to strangers, suppliants at my door,
> not even heralds out on their public errands here—
> I yearn for Odysseus, always, my heart pines away. (394)

Yet Penelope is never a central character in *The Odyssey* as her presentation is limited by her stereotypical domesticity. Similarly, Hera's depiction is based on her being the goddess of married women. In many myths, Hera's power is tested on women, especially on those who have love affairs with Zeus. Hera is mostly praised as the "golden-throned" and "white-armed" Goddess. Although her power is close to Zeus's, in the following address to Zeus, Hera recognizes the source of her power as her relation to two male gods: her father Kronos and her husband Zeus.

> I too am a god, and of the same descent as you:
> I am the senior of all daughters born to devious-minded Kronos,
> for double reason, both by birth and because I am called your wife,
> and you are the lord of all immortals. (54)

Joseph Campbell suggests that it is mythologically grounded that a girl becomes a woman automatically by menstruation, marriage and giving birth whereas the boy has to search for his manhood (168). Campbell supports his idea with references to the divine call made to Telemachus in the *Odyssey*: "Young man, go find your father" (Campbell 168). This argument may account for men's active and women's passive presence in Western myths. Another issue driven from Campbell's argument is that women are always there, at home. Thus children never have to search for their maternal backgrounds. In this respect, it is once more asserted that women are depicted as domestic characters, with their limited experience in social life. In other words, they are either daughters or wives and/or mothers.

Furthermore ethnic and/or national backgrounds have a significant place in these myths since these myths explore power relations between the master and the slave, the superior versus the subordinate, the intruder versus the victim; or broadly speaking the oppressor and the oppressed. The notion of exile, too, serves as a significant element implying oppression in Western myths. The royal houses of Atreus (to which Agamemnon and his family belong), Thebes (the place of origin of Oedipus and his family) and Athens all inspire rivalry between heroes and thus witness many searches for power and dominance. For instance in *The Iliad*, Hector and Achilles's long-lasting fight may be taken as such a sign of power struggle.

Early Greek writings may be considered among the milestones of Western literature since there are still many references to them. Besides, the Greek myths are placed at the core of literature syllabi which account for Eurocentricity in the literary canon. While early Greek writings involve gender, class and ethnic oppressions thematically as significant elements, their Western structures also reflect oppression through their form. In this respect Euripides' *Medea* and Sophocles' *Oedipus the King, Oedipus at Colonus* may be suggested among the examplary texts of early Greek power structures.

3.1. Signs of Oppression in Euripides' *Medea*

Euripides' tragedy *Medea* embodies striking power structures based on dominance and oppression such as master versus servant, male versus female, native versus foreigner and finally adult versus child. In *Medea*, Euripides introduces a gradually defamiliarizing land which once witnessed the strong love between Jason and his wife Medea. As the land is ruled by King Creon with absolute power, the citizens have become no different from slaves. As for the foreigners, the situation is even worse. For instance Jason is about to marry Creon's daughter just to hold some power and Medea is destined to exiled if she rebels.

The play opens as the Chorus, consisting of Corinthian women, reminds Medea and the reader/audience of the past when Medea betrayed her own fatherland for the sake of Jason. Although Medea is threatened by Creon and Jason, she pursues a wild plan to avenge Jason's betrayal. While she pretends to reconcile herself with them, she sends the bride a poisoned gift. Tragically, she victimizes her own children as instruments of her revenge, opposing the stereotypical mother role.

In *Medea,* Euripides portrays tyrannical rule in Corinth where decisions are made only by the King and are never questioned. When Creon is first introduced, he orders Medea to leave the city (R. Warner translation).

> You with that angry look, so set against your husband,
> Medea, I order you to leave my territories
> An exile, and take along with you your two children,
> And not to waste time doing it. It is my decree,
> And I will see it done. I will not return home
> Until you are cast from the boundaries of my land. (19)

Creon has so assertive a tone that it never softens even after Medea asks him the reason for this order. Furthermore the following lines suggest that Creon's reason for sending Medea away is very personal: "I am afraid of you—why should I dissemble it?— Afraid that you may injure my daughter mortally" (20).

Although such a personal attitude is not expected from a king, later on Creon himself accounts for his choice between his country and his personal life as such: "I love my country too—next, after my children" (22). In this respect, Creon's rule might be considered tyrannical since his lines imply that he views his citizens as secondary to his royal family. That Creon is willing to use his absolute power is also put forth when he threatens to send Medea away by force if she does not leave Corinth herself (11). Even though Creon claims "[t]here is nothing tyrannical about my nature" (23), his tyrannical nature is once more asserted in Jason's lines to Medea:

> For, with reasonable submission to our ruler's will,
> You might have lived in this land and kept your home.
> As it is you are going to be exiled for your loose speaking.
> Not that I mind myself. You are free to continue
> Telling everyone that Jason is a worthless man.
> But as to talk about the king, consider
> Yourself most lucky that exile is your punishment. (26)

Jason's lines state that Medea is being sent away for no action but words. That Jason is afraid of the king is explicit in the last four lines of the above quote. Furthermore, Jason implies that he views the king as more important than himself, which in turn accounts for his royal marriage.

In "Medea In Corinth: Political Aspects of Euripides' *Medea*," C. A. E. Luschnig also argues that Creon is a tyrant in many ways. The following lines further explain the ways of Creon's tyranny: "Creon is not the worst of tyrants, a man with insatiable appetites, but he is drawn as one who assumes a master's power over the households of the city and who acts like a god in determining the fates of the residents" (8).

Besides, the system is thoroughly patriarchal as women are instruments of men's search for power. For instance both Medea and the princess serve as the bystanders of Jason's future plans. In his conversation with Medea, Jason expresses his disrespect for women:

> It would have been better far for men
> To have got their children in some other way, and women
> Not to have existed. Then life would have been good. (30)

Furthermore, in the following lines, Jason sets his pragmatic reasons for his new marriage.

> Make sure of this: it was not because of a woman
> I made the royal alliance in which I now live,
> But, as I said before, I wished to preserve you
> And breed a royal progeny to be brothers
> To the children I have now, a sure defense to us. (31)

While Medea suffers for the loss of her husband, the princess is to lose even her life; both for the sake of Jason's individualistic concerns. In this respect, both women are being oppressed by their common husband.

Similarly the Corinthian women, who in Euripides' *Medea* stand for the traditional Greek Chorus, reflect the oppressed situation of women in those times of Greek society. While the Corinthian women at times empathize with Medea—"This I will promise. You are in the right, Medea,/ In paying your husband back. I am not surprised at you/ For being sad" (19)—sometimes they state that with her cruelty, Medea may not be taken as a representative woman but only as an exception.

> Of one alone I have heard, one woman alone
> Of those of old who laid her hands on her children,
> Ino, sent mad by heaven when the wife of Zeus
> Drove her out from her home and made her wander;
> And because of the wicked shedding of blood
> Of her own children she threw
> Herself, poor wretch, into the sea and stepped away
> Over the sea-cliff to die with her two children. (58)

The above lines imply that there has been only one more woman who is as cruel as Medea and even she could not bear the sorrow of killing her own children and finally comitted suicide. Similarly, the Nurse, as a representative of the Corinthian women, calls Medea "a strange woman" (9) because she sacrificed her own family for the love of Jason. This implies their distanced perspective towards Medea.

Although the chorus of Corinthian women too are against male rule,

> Flow backward to your sources, sacred rivers,
> And let the world's great order be reversed.
> It is the thought of *men* that are deceitful,
> *Their* pledges that are too loose. (25)

they might be considered to be themselves conformist characters.

> Since you have shared the knowlege of your plan with us,
> I both wish to help you and support the normal
> Ways of mankind, and tell you not to do this thing. (41)

The Corinthian women experience a great conflict in their approach towards Medea. While Medea appeals to their repressed warrior spirits, she is at the same time the wife with children and interestingly, the passionate woman. Thus from the Corinthian women's perspective Medea might be considered as ambiguous. On the other hand, the Corinthian women's final reconciliation with the existing male order, just before the curtain, might be viewed in feminist wording, as internalized patriarchy. The following lines imply how they consolidate with existing patriarchal power structures.

> Zeus in Olympus is the overseer
> Of many doings. Many things the gods
> Achieve beyond our judgement. What we thought
> Is not confirmed and what we thought not god
> Contrives. And so it happens in the story. (64)

The above lines suggest that the Corinthian women accept the dominance of a male god, Zeus, which in turn stands for a continuing male order as they have finally stopped waiting for the goddess they used to expect:

> Often before
> I have gone through more subtle reasons,
> And have come upon questionings greater
> Than a woman should strive to search out.
> But we too have a goddess to help us
> And accompany us into wisdom. (51, 52)

From another perspective, the final reconciliation with the chief Olympian god, Zeus, also implies a master/slave relationship in which men are to be obeyed, not questioned. The idea that Zeus is the overseer leads to a notion of being limited in action. That's why the hierarchal order of god-hero and common man is once more centralized in the play.

Medea stands as a female rebel only because she feels resentful after too much oppression. Otherwise she might be a stereotypically submissive woman figure who is willing to victimize her identity for her husband's sake. For instance, in one of her early addresses to the women of Corinth, Medea seems to have internalized the conventional role of women.

> Of all things which are living and can form a judgement
> We women are the most unfortunate creatures.
> Firstly, with an excess of wealth it is required
> For us to buy a husband and take for our bodies
> A master, for not to take one is even worse. (18)

The fact that Medea once betrayed her own family for Jason, also supports the idea that she used to favour Jason over her very self.

On the other hand, Medea experiences oppression not only as a citizen and a woman but also as an outsider who lacks both rootedness and relatedness in the city of Corinth. As the nurse notes at the very beginning of the play "There is no home" for Medea (14). In her address to the Corinthian women, Medea also considers herself an outsider in the land: "Women of Corinth, I have come outside to you" (17). In the following lines, she further suggests that as a foreigner, she has neither roots nor relations in this land:

> You have a country. Your family home is here.
> You enjoy life and the company of your friends.
> But I am deserted, a refugee, thought nothing of
> By my husband—something he won in a foreign land.
> I have no mother or brother, nor any relation
> With whom I can take refuge in this sea of woe. (18, 19)

The Chorus consisting of Corinthian women assert Medea's difficult situation as a foreigner in the following lines which they utter after Creon tells Medea to leave the country:

> Oh, unfortunate one! Oh, cruel!
> Where will you turn? Who will help you?
> What house or what land to preserve you
> From ill can you find? (23)

Even though Medea truly resents this triple oppression, her revolt ends up initiating another form of oppression. Since the oppressor always oppresses the ones who have less power than him/her, Medea adheres to this system of oppression and oppresses her children; the only ones she can test her power on. In her article entitled "After *Oedipus*: *Laius*, *Medea* and Other Parental Myths," Nancy Datan considers *Medea* among the myths that exemplify "the willingness of parents to sacrifice children in the service of self." (17) Based on her argument, it is possible to suggest that each and every oppressor sacrifices his/her oppressed in the service of him/herself. In this respect, Medea follows the same path as her oppressor Jason and victimizes her children for her own reasons.

> I have no land, no home, or refuge from my pain.
> My mistake was made the time I left behind me
> My father's house, and trusted the words of a Greek,
> Who, with heaven's help, will pay me the price for that.
> For those childen he had from me he will never
> See alive again, nor will he on his new bride
> Beget another child, for she is to be forced
> To die a terrible death by these my poisons. (41)

Hence, it is possible to read *Medea* as a myth involving different types of oppression. Despite the numerous criticisms which view Medea as a female rebel, a study of the reasons lying beneath the rebel locates Medea within the dialectics of oppressor/ oppressed. With a multitude of segments of her identity, Medea is exposed to oppression in many ways which in turn announce her rebellion, more out of resentment than anything else.

The English word resentment derives from the French *ressentiment* which, in the context of the study of self and other, has become a literary-critical term. The word was originally used by Nietzsche in his *Genealogy of Morals* where he specifically argues that the ancient Jews had feelings of *ressentiment* against the more powerful Romans (1969: 33). Nietzsche further notes that with the feeling of *ressentiment,* the slaves called their enemies, the Romans, evil, a term reflecting their "submerged hatred, the vengefulness of the impotent" (1969: 37-38). To Nietzsche, what caused *ressentiment* was the power dynamics between the impotent Jews and the prepotent Romans as well as the sense of frustration that the awareness of such an unequal situation entails. Nietzsche finally argues that evoking revenge, *ressentiment* causes an "inversion of the traditional value system" (39, 40).

Following Nietzsche, Frantz Fanon traces the word to his understanding of the colonized subject who also has *ressentiment* since he/she wishes the destruction of the domination of the master, the colonizer. To set the argument in Fanon's words in *Wretched of The Earth*, "The gaze that the colonized subject casts at the colonist's sector is a look of lust, a look of envy, dreams of possession. The colonized man is an envious man" (2004: 5). Another theorist who worked on the concept of *ressentiment* is Max Scheler who also suggests that "uncontrolled powerful feelings in subordination" such as "hatred, revenge, malice, envy and spite" can finally lead to *ressentiment* which he defines as "a dangerous poisoning of the mind and the soul" (Scheler, 2003: 25).

In this respect, it is possible to view *Medea* as a myth of oppression which finally ends up in powerful feelings of *ressentiment*. As too much oppression ultimately causes *ressentiment,* the oppressed Medea is given the motivation to avenge her oppressor Jason. However, her resentful revenge leads to an inversion of values, from a Nietzschean perspective, since the formerly oppressed Medea becomes the oppressor in relation to both her own children and Jason's new wife.

3.2. Sophocles' *The Theban Plays* in Relation to Oppression

The myth of Oedipus involves similar signs of oppression which go parallel to *ressentiment*. In both *Oedipus the King* and *Oedipus at Colonus*, Sophocles employs the theme of child oppression by parents as well as class and gender oppression. Similar to *Medea*'s situation in Corinth, Oedipus is both a foreigner and a native in Thebes. As he comes to the land from outside, he is a stranger, yet since he is the biological child of the king and the queen of Thebes, he is a statesman. After being exposed to different types of oppression, Oedipus also resents his fate truly and he blinds himself.

In *Oedipus The King*, the plague in Thebes is very central to the initial scene. Oedipus, the Priest and Creon are after the reasons for such a curse. When they initially find out that the land is cursed by gods because of the hidden murder of the former king, Laius, Oedipus decides to find the murderer. Ironically he is to find out that he is the murderer himself. Later he also learns that the prophecy that he is destined to kill his own father and marry his own mother has come true. When eventually he understands that his wife Jocasta is his biological mother, Jocasta has already learned the truth and commits suicide. To punish himself, Oedipus blinds himself and asks the new king Creon to send him to exile.

There are many representations of the oppressor and the oppressed in Sophocles' play *Oedipus The King*. It is revealed that after hearing the oracle about their baby son, the parents wish him dead. This is a significant sign of child oppression by its parents. While they victimize their child, the child has to keep silent and play the oppressed. This situation is reminiscent of Nany Datan's argument in "After *Oedipus*: *Lauis*, *Medea* and Other Parental Myths," since Oedipus is another example of parents's sacrifice of their children to preserve their ego. (17) In his psychoanalytic reading of *Oedipus Rex*, Bruno Bettelheim suggests that Oedipus's parents, Lauis and Jocasta, had the choice of not believing in the oracle. He further argues that Lauis chose to sacrifice his son as the son would replace him. To Bettelheim, the fact that Jocasta does nothing to protect her son is because she is afraid that she would love the son more than the husband. (28) Based on Bettelheim's views, it may be claimed that the child is exposed to his parents's oppression for their individual concerns. Since he is not an adult, he cannot yet resist this oppression.

However, Jocasta's representation is ambiguous in the play. Whether she contributed to the plan directly or indirectly by keeping silent, is the central question. There are suggestions in the play that the decision was made by others and the mother, Jocasta, had to obey: "Apollo was explicit: my son was doomed to kill my husband… my son, poor defenseless thing, he never had a chance to kill his father. They destroyed him first" (208). Besides, as the queen of Thebes, Jocasta had no choice but to marry Oedipus who solved the riddle of Sphinx and saved the country. Because Jocasta commits suicide after learning that Oedipus is her son, she might be considered another victim. As a sign of patriarchy in the play, all the rulers and decision-makers (Apollo, Teiresias, Lauis, Oedipus, Creon) are male. Even though she is the queen, Jocasta hardly has more than a bystander's position in the play.

On the other hand, the Olympian god Apollo is presented in such a way as to recall the hierarchical order of gods, heroes and other men. The notion of fate which goes parallel to the oracle also implies the dialectics of self and the other. The Olympian gods who decide men's destiny are the Other of men. The following lines of the Chorus (in Robert Fagles's translation) support this idea:

> Destiny guide me always
> Destiny find me filled with reverence
> pure in word and deed.
> Great laws tower above us, reared on high
> born for the brilliant vault of heaven—
> Olympian Sky their only father,
> nothing mortal, no man gave them birth,
> their memory deathless, never lost in sleep:
> within them lives a mighty god, the god does not
> grow old. (209)

Apollo and the blind prophet Teiresias, whom the leader believes he can see "with the eyes of Apollo" (174), both function as the Other of Oedipus who is oppressed by their oracle.

> Apollo, friends, Apollo—
> he ordained my agonies—these, my pains on pains!
> But the hand that struck my eyes was mine,
> mine alone—no one else—
> I did it all myself. (241)

With the revelation of the past, Oedipus is thus estranged from himself and becomes his own enemy. Another representation of the Other in the play is the Sphinx who, through the riddle, oppresses the whole country and serves as an instrument for the fall of Oedipus. In this respect, there are power structures higher than the king which in turn make him oppressed. That Oedipus is never free to make a choice as he is limited by the oracle, supports this argument.

There is also certainly a hierarchal order based on class in the play. As the only power-holder, the king is the tyrant. As the Chorus notes "Pride breeds the tyrant" (209). Oedipus's tyranny goes parallel to his pride. Although in *Oedipus The King*, there are also some implications of a democratic order at least among Oedipus, Jocasta and Creon, (192, 193) the following words by the Priest, who calls Oedipus "our greatest power" (160), describe Oedipus's highly privileged situation:

> Now we pray to you. You cannot equal the gods,
> your children know that, bending at your altar.
> But we do rate you first of men,
> both in the common crises of our lives
> and face-to-face encounters with the gods. (161)

The Priest's words also support the idea that there is definitely a representation of a hierarchal order in the play. Bernard Knox considers Oedipus "the enforcer of law" (141). To Knox, Oedipus is also "the investigator, prosecutor and judge of a murder" (141). Although Knox relates these aspects of Oedipus's ruling to an early imperial democracy, there is hardly any sign of democracy in the play. For instance in his conversation with Teiresias, Oedipus addresses Teiresias as a superior. Calling Teiresas "You, you scum of the earth," Oedipus forces him to reveal the murderer: "You are bound to tell me that" (178). Oedipus's tone is so assertive that Teiresias has to remind him that he is not Oedipus's slave:

> You are the king no doubt, but in one respect,
> at least I am your equal: the right to reply.
> I claim that privilege too.
> I am not your slave. I serve Apollo. (183)

Even in his conversation with Creon, Oedipus displays a similar attitude:

> Creon: What do you want?
> You want me banished?
> Oedipus: No, I want you dead. (194)

Thus, it may be claimed that Oedipus likes to test his power on the less privileged. This might be taken as a sign of his oppressive side whereas he is also oppressed by the more powerful ones. When everything is revealed and Oedipus blinds himself, the new king Creon does not oppose Oedipus's wish to be sent away. However Creon reminds Oedipus that Oedipus is no longer the powerful one.

> Still the king, the master of all things?
> No more: here your power ends.
> None of your power follows you through life. (250)

Oedipus's experience in exile is represented in Sophocles' *Oedipus At Colonus*, another Theban play, in which Oedipus is exposed to further oppression. As he leaves Thebes, Oedipus, accompanied by his daughter Antigone, reaches Colonus which is close to Athens. Oedipus becomes the oppressed in this, the second play, since, in exile, he is no more than a cursed stranger. He is an outsider not only because he is blind and non-native but also because he has an embarrassing past. In his first lines Oedipus implies that he is prepared to be subordinate to the natives:

> ... We have come
> to learn from the citizens, strangers from citizens,
> and carry out their wishes to the end. (283)

As in his encounter with a citizen of Colonus, Oedipus is forbidden to walk on the holy ground, he accepts the situation and just asks for the names of the Ones to pray to them (285). In this respect, what Oedipus seeks in this foreign land is not authority but merely reconciliation. Yet the Citizen who addresses Oedipus as "old stranger," (287) also adds that they have nothing to gain from a blind man (288). Similarly the Chorus first calls Oedipus "A wanderer, wandering fugitive / that old man—no native, a stranger (291); later "blind, blind, poor man" (292), and finally, when they learn that he is Oedipus, the Chorus exclaims, "Out with you! Out of our country—far away!" (297). Oedipus is exposed to oppression for each and every of his differences.

Oedipus's next encounter is with his daughter Ismene who tells him and Antigone about the rivalry between Oedipus's two sons (Polynices, Eteocles) for the succession to the throne after Creon. Oedipus further learns from Ismene that Oedipus's sons prefer power to the chance of bringing their father back to their homeland. At this, Oedipus is full of *ressentiment*:

> No, no, may the great gods
> never quench their blazing, fated strife!
> May it rest in my hands alone—
> now their spears are lifting tip to tip—
> to bring their fighting to its bitter end.
> I'd see that the one who holds the scepter now
> would not last long, nor would the outcast
> ever return again! When I, their own father
> was doomed off native ground, disgraced
> they didn't lift a finger, didn't defend me, no,
> they just looked on, they watched me driven from home,
> they heard the heralds cry my sentence-exile! (309)

It may be concluded that Oedipus is oppressed by his sons as well. While they have the power to change his destiny, they prefer to victimize him. The reason why Oedipus may be considered the oppressed is because he never truly had an unlimited freedom of choice and yet he had to bear the consequences of an unmade choice. His address to the Chorus supports this idea:

> I have suffered, friends,
> the worst horrors on earth, suffered against my will,
> I swear to god, not a single thing, self-willed— (315)

Oedipus is also oppressed by Creon who sentences Oedipus to death and wants to take his two daughters away. Noting that he is "innocent," Oedipus utters the following lines which once again reveal his oppression:

> Come, tell me: if, by an oracle of the gods,
> some doom were hanging over my father's head
> that he should die at the hands of his own son,
> how, with any justice, could you blame me?
> I wasn't born yet, no father implanted me,
> No mother carried me in her womb—
> I didn't even exist, not then! And if,
> once I have come to the world of pain, as come I did,
> fell to blows with my father, cut him down in blood—
> blind to what I was doing, blind to whom I killed—
> how could you condemn that involuntary actwith any sense of justice? (344)

When Oedipus finally dies at Colonus, he has only his two daughters and Theseus, the king of Colonus, to remember his name. Tragically, he was finally able to make a choice at least about his death if not about his life. As Antigone notes, "He has died on foreign soil, the soil of his choice..." (384). Since Oedipus belonged nowhere, he died in exile, as the Other to both Thebes and Colonus.

3.3. Structures of Oppression and the Aristotelian Tradition

There is a noteworthy parallelism among the above considered examples of early Greek plays in terms of their content, which displays oppression. These plays also use technique to announce oppression as they are meant for an audience that risks gradually internalizing the frequently represented hierarchical, ethnic and gender oppression. Since oppression is displayed as a very recurrent pattern in classical theatre, it may gradually be misconceived as the norm.

The Brazilian theater critic, Augusto Boal, argues that, in adhering to the Aristotelian tradition, the classical theatre contains oppressive codes and structures, especially through *empathy* and *catharsis* which respectively lead to the audience's identification with the protagonist and purification through the protagonist's suffering due to his tragic flaw or *hamartia* (38). Boal describes the process through which the Aristotelian tradition operates towards *catharsis* as follows:

> -*Peripeteia*: *Hamartia* is evoked; the audience empathizes with the protagonist, the audience accompanies the protagonist intially to the peak and later to his downfall.
>
> -*Anagnorisis:* As the protogonist recognizes his flaw, the audience recognizes his own flaw, his own *hamartia*, or his own illegal behavior through the emphatic relationship between dianoia (taking action) and reason.
>
> -*Catastrophe*: The protagonist is made to bear the tragic consequences of his action.
>
> *Catharsis*: As the audience witnesses the catastrophe and feels pity and terror, he is purified from his own hamartia.

Since this system finally directs the audience to social *ethos*, the audience is systematically made to conform with the social values and rules, his/her individual *ethos* being oppressed (Boal 39-47). Thus Boal argues that the traditional understanding of theatre has an explicitly "political" concern in introducing such a "system of oppression." (1-4) Boal uses the above mentioned system to analyze the process Oedipus goes through. Boal suggests that Sophocles provides the perfect social *ethos* through the Chorus and Teiresias. However, to Boal, a conflict between *hamartia* and social ethos arises as Oedipus, due to his pride, does not accept his guilt despite Teiresias's announcement of it. His pride is the source of both his initial power and later downfall. As the audience witnesses the tragic consequences through the representation of the suicide of Oedipus's mother/wife, catastrophe takes place and then leads to catharsis (Boal 39-40).

Boal offers five different types of conflicts between *hamartia* and social *ethos*, namely *hamartia* versus perfect social *ethos* (the classical one, Oedipus's case), *hamartia* versus *hamartia* and the two *hamartia*s versus perfect social *ethos*, negative *hamartia* versus perfect social *ethos*, negative *hamartia* versus negative social *ethos* and finally anachronic individual *ethos* versus contemporary social *ethos* (39-45). However Boal notes that it is the former two which strictly follow the Aristotelian rules (39-41) and exemplifies the second type through *Antigone*.

The cases of many male protagonists may be associated with the first type while for the female protagonist, the second type seems to be a better match. Boal's classification of *hamartia* versus perfect social *ethos* requires the protagonist to be at the very center of the play. In other words, the protagonist needs to be the agent of the central action and thus be responsible for the tragic consequences of his own acting or decision. For instance, Oedipus is the leading force of the tragedy since he, through in his ignorance, killed Laius and married Jocasta. In other words, he is the agent or subject of the action which leads to the tragedy.

As for the second type, hamartia versus hamartia and the two hamartias versus perfect social ethos, Boal gives the example of *Antigone* in which he considers the hamartias of Antigone (excessive love for her brother) and Creon (excessive love for his country) as conflicting (40). Boal further suggests that this play requires the audience to empathize with both of the characters since the audience has to be purified from both hamartias (40). However Boal does not focus on a possible relationship between gender and the second type. It may not be coincidental that the two major tragedies named after their female protagonists fit into Type Two which involves a second *hamartia;* thus, an alternative protagonist. In other words, the protagonists of the tragedies in Type Two are not as priviledged as those of Type One, in being situated at the centre of their tragedies. For instance in *Antigone*, Antigone is hardly an agent or a decisionmaker in her own tragedy which ends with her suicide. Antigone is neither the agent of the fight between her two brothers nor is she the traitor herself. Yet Creon can make a decision by offering her a dilemma between two undesirable choices: She would either leave her brother (whom Creon announces as a traitor) unburied or be exiled. Building on the feminist definition of oppression offered in Chapter 1, one can suggest that Antigone is oppressed and even victimized in her own tragedy. Similarly in *Medea*, Medea is not the only source of her action. What directs her to her hamartia is her blind passion for revenge which is her tragic flaw. However Medea's hamartia is not the only one leading to the tragedy. Without Jason's adultery and ambition, the chain of events would not have taken place.

In both tragedies with female protagonists, their *hamartia*s conflict initially with those alternative, male, protagonists, and later with the Chorus which traditionally calls for the internalization of the conventional system or work for "the perfect social *ethos,*" borrowing from Boal (39). To be more precise, the female-specific version of Boal's model can be offered below:

-The disobedience of the female protagonist (hamartia or individual ethos) against the will of the male authority and the conventions (social ethos)
-Her initial rise through her disobedience (Medea's disobedience to her own father for Jason or Antigone's disobedience to Creon for her brother); witnessed by the reader/audience which leads to empathy and then her fall

due to excessive disobedience
-Purification through her suffering, which in turn leads to catharsis.

By way of another example, the Apollo-Marsyas myth reflects a master-and-slave relationship in telling the story of a deity sentencing a mortal severely for daring to challenge the deity's authority. According to the legend, Marsyas, a mortal, challenges Apollo to a contest of music and loses the contest, judged by the Muses. As the winner is free to treat the loser any way he wants, Apollo decides to flay Marsyas alive in a cave. Apollo then nails Marsyas' skin to a pine tree near a lake. Nursel İçöz considers the Apollo-Marsyas myth in "Domestic Violence in *The Black Prince*" as a sign of "considerable violence" (42). As violence inevitably leads to physical oppression, it is also possible to read the myth as a myth of oppression. The myth may be related to a hierarchical oppression, especially, since Marsyas is oppressed by Apollo as his body becomes a tool for Apollo's assertion of his divine authority. According to Boal's suggestion of an involvement of a system of oppression in the Aristotelian tradition, which is discussed in Chapter 3, the Apollo-Marsyas myth follows the same pattern of oppression in its form:

- Marsyas's ambition (hamartia or individual ethos) against Apollo who signifies divine obedience (social ethos).
- His initial rise in music and his later fall in music; witnessed by the reader which leads to empathy.
- Purification through Marsyas's penalty which leads to catharsis.

In this respect, the Apollo-Marsyas myth makes the reader gradually witness the rise and fall of Marsyas due to his ambition and focuses on the tragic outcome of his excessive ambition which makes him challenge an authority. In other words, the myth may be considered a positive reinforcer of oppressive power structures by displaying the tragic consequences of disobedience to authorities.

The Demeter and Persephone myth implies the involvement of a noteworthy gender oppression in Greek myths. In the Demeter and Persephone myth, Demeter's daughter Persephone (by Zeus) became the consort of Hades, the god of the underworld. Demeter was capable of destroying all life on earth as she controlled the seasons. She used all her power on Zeus and Zeus made Hades bring their daughter back. When one day Persephone was picking flowers, a great chasm opened up behind her and Hades took her back to the Underworld. As Demeter hopelessly searched for her lost daughter, life on earth stopped. Finally, Zeus had to ask Hades to return Persephone. Hades agreed to send her up only if she had not eaten any food in the underworld. Yet Persephone had already eaten six pomegranate seeds, due to which she had to return to the underworld for six months each year. When Demeter and her daughter were together, the earth became fertile. When Persephone returned to the underworld, the earth became barren. The Demeter and Persephone myth displays the conventional mother-daughter relationship as protective and fragile, in turn as active and passive; even as intrusive and obedient, respectively. Demeter challenges her daughter's will to be with a man and displays the mother's conventional search for authority over her children. On the other hand Hades is able to decide Persephone's fate. In this respect, Persephone is oppressed by both her mother and Hades who, together with Zeus, stand for patriarchy.

Similarly, the myth of Philomela foregrounds a significant instance of the oppression of a woman. The myth centrally deals with Philomela's rape by her brother-in-law and her revenge. Philomela, the princess of Athens, is the sister of Procne who is married to Tereus, king of Thrace. One day Procne asks Tereus to escort Philomela to Thrace for a visit. When they arrive at their destination, Tereus rapes Philomela in a cabin in the woods. Because she says she will tell everybody he raped her, Tereus cuts her tongue out. Philomela then weaves a robe that tells her story and sends it to Procne. In revenge, Procne kills her son Itys and serves him to his father. When Tereus discovers that he's eaten his own son, he tries to kill Philomela and Procne. Changed into birds (nightingales, in some versions) by Olympic gods, the two sisters fly away. The myth of Philomela explores women's physical oppression by men by setting forth that man views female body as an object. Given this context, Tereus's cutting Philomela's tongue out indicates also an emotional oppression as it implies women's being silenced by men under patriarchy.

In this respect, it is possible to consider the above analyzed myths of oppression as both reflections and reinforcers of inevitable power structures in early Western civilizations. These myths display ethnic, hierarchal and gender oppression not only in their content but also through their form and structure which indirectly contribute to the continuum of this system. The canonization and standardization of these myths, on the other hand, have gradually introduced a broader notion of oppression which is to be discussed in Chapter 4.

4. Ethnic Roots Retraced

Since Western myths have always been the center of literary attention, all introductory courses to world literature inevitably involve Greek and Roman myths in their syllabi. Western literature has always been on the agenda while the so-called Third World literatures are neglected. In his work entitled *Literary Theory: An Introduction*, Terry Eagleton argues that literature inevitably reflects the current social ideologies and its reader brings it a conventional context which reconciles with the major patterns through which privileged social groups "exercise and maintain power over others." (1-14) From a Marxist perspective, Eagleton specifically focuses on English literature as a case study and traces the reason why it was popularized, in an attempt to control the agenda among the working classes and women, in his chapter entitled "The Rise of English" (23-37). Drawing upon Eagleton's argument, one may suggest that literature has been a tool to reinforce the dialectics of self and Other in all possible aspects.

As noted in Chapter 2, recent postcolonial studies have brought the issue of Western canonization into discussion. For instance, Gayatri C. Spivak traces the relationship between English and Gikuyu to "the relationship between *dominant* literature and subordinate *orature*" (Spivak, 1996: 238). Similarly, the Chicano critic Ramon Salvidar suggests that both Chicano literature and literary criticism "have been excluded from the traditional framework of American literature" (Calderon and Salvidar 11). In his introduction to *Gendering The Nation: Studies In Modern Scottish Literature*, Christopher Wyte also mentions the oppositions to the canonization of Scottish literature (x). In this respect, the current postcolonial arguments state that indigenous literatures have long been neglected within the broader scope of so–called world literature.

Therefore postcolonial critics ask for the canonization of indigenous literatures and their use in literature course syllabi. For instance, in his book entitled *Signifying Monkey and The Afro-American Literary Tradition*, Henry Louis Gates owns this perspective as he searches for the authentic roots of black vernacular tradition so as to find a systematic relationship between African American texts. Similar to Gates, Ramon Salvidar calls for the recognition of Mexican American writing as a different tradition of writing. (11, 12) The following words of G.C. Spivak imply a similar call:

> [W]e should have to consider the millennially suppressed oral cultures of the aboriginals of India. We have not yet seen an Indo-Anglican fiction writer of tribal origin; we are far from seeing one who has gone back to his or her own oral heritage. (1996: 238)

Christopher Whyte celebrates the emerging of Scottish literature "from under the shadows of English literature" as well as its establishing a specific canon (x). The following lines by Uma Narayan and Sandra Harding indicate the same search for reconciliation between Euro-centric and Other traditions by suggesting a revision of all notions of Western hegemony.

> As the "Others" of modernity's ideal humans—such as women, and peoples of non-European races and cultures—increasingly are recognized as fully human, we should expect transformations in the fundamental landscapes of Western metaphysics, epistemology, ethics, political philosophy, and even philosophies of science. (ix)

All these theorists with different ethnic backgrounds work on canonizing and foregrounding such literatures of different ethnic origins which, otherwise, will always be the Others of Western literature. Among the English-speaking cultures, the Irish, Scottish, Welsh, Asian British/American, African British/African American and Chicano(a)/Latino(a) literatures need further consideration. In order to exemplify different ethnic backgrounds in British and American literatures, Scottish and Celtic myths which significantly shape the Scottish writing tradition will be foregrounded as well as Mayan and Aztec myths which greatly influence the Chicano(a) / Latino(a) literatures.

4.1. A Background on Scottish, Celtic and Aztec, Mayan Myths

Although Celtic tradition dates back to the 4th Century B.C, no Celtic mythology was recorded before the Christian era. Irish, Welsh and Scottish cultures can be considered among the heirs of the old Celtic civilizations. Celtic mythology possesses an interestingly hybrid quality as it embodies the whole of Indo-European culture, including the Hindu and the Hitite.

Old Irish used to be the old standard literary language of the Gaelic-speaking world until the late Medieval period. Manx and Scots diverged from this family. Therefore there are similar myths and legends among the survivors of the old Celtic tradition, namely in Ireland, the Isle of Man and Scotland.

While oral story-telling makes up for the most significant characteristic of Celtic culture, Celtic myths are noted to depict "a world of fantasy which is remote from the world of Greek and Latin..." (Ellis 19). Celtic myths involve an eternal optimism since there is no end to life. Thus, immortality of the soul versus death and reincarnation are among the most recurrent elements in Celtic myths. It is noted that deities in Celtic myths are depicted more as ancestors of people than their creators (Ellis 21). It may be suggested that the Celts' optimistic attitude toward death possibly leads to a different conception of deities, not as Others, but as part of themselves. Since there is no fear of death for human beings, Celtic gods and goddesses are not viewed as privileged immortals, unlike the Greek and Roman ones.

The Scottish myths adhere to the Celtic ones in terms of their conception of the deities. In Scottish myths, the deities and other supernatural characters have peaceful relations with human beings and there is nothing like the oppressive structure in Greek and Roman myths. In contrast to the Greek and Roman gods that often punish men, the Scottish deities take a mission to "instruct and delight" the human beings through art. In both Celtic and Scottish myths, goddesses are more significant than gods. The Celtic goddess Danu is known to be the first deity. In Wales, the fairies represent the Earth Mothers who are identified with nurturing and protection. Similarly, all rivers of Scotland are associated with specific goddesses. Beira, the Queen of Winter, is recognized as the mother of all Scottish gods and goddesses. Season has great importance in Scottish myths and legends, as the climate in Scotland is rather harsh. In winter the peaks of mountains are covered with snow and many lochs are frozen. The Scottish people believed that during the reign of Beira, the Queen of Winter, the Spirit of Spring was trying to visit Scotland and "they imagined that Beira raised the storms of January and February to prolong her reign by keeping the grass from growing" (MacKenzie 10). In many Scottish legends, Beira was depicted as a cruel and strict old woman. It is believed that she formed the lochs and the mountains. There are also female water spirits shaping the weather conditions such as Gentle Annie, Bride and the lady of summer growth.

MacKenzie's argument about the Scottish belief that there were mysterious powers or a power greater than that of gods and goddesses (14) is exemplified with references to Beira who might raise storms and bring snow but who still could not prevent the grass from growing in spring (15). In this respect even the divine power is limited by the order of nature which is similar to the Egyptian conception of nature as the central force. In Egyptian myths and legends, nature unites and protects all creatures which are believed to be her own reflections. The fact that in Scottish and Celtic myths there is a similar notion of recycling and reincarnating nature may account for the lack of hierarchy between the deities and human beings.

Another mythology built on the regenerative powers of nature is that of the Aztecs. The native language of the Aztec is known to be Nahuatl. Aztecs who had both military and economic power, overshadowed other Nahuatl groups such as Texcocans, Cholulaw, Chalcans and Tlaxcaltecs. They all settled around the Gulf of Mexico on the Pacific Ocean during the fifteenth and sixteenth centuries. The Nahuas (ancient Mexicans) had a common cultural heritage which inspired the Spaniards. The early Nahuatl texts dealt with "the human destiny on earth" as well as "the fugacity of life" (Leon-Portilla viii).

Cosmological myths are viewed as the basis of Nahuatl philosophy and religion (Leon-Portilla xxi). The Nahua records show that they were good at sculpture, architecture and pictograph manuscripts. Further studies demonstrate that the Nahuas then had an exact science of time, a complex religion, a just but strict law system as well as medical and military skills. Leon-Portilla suggests that there are two aspects of Nahuatl culture "which have been neglected all too long-literature and philosophy" (xxii). He adds that, as with the Greeks, among the Nahuas it was first the lyric poets who focused on the dilemmas of human existence (xxiii). In this respect it is interesting to note that Nahuatl poetry which dealt with such philosophical questioning was hardly brought on the agenda. However, it is noted that according to the Nahuas, poetry is the only way man can communicate with the Divine (Leon-Portilla 79).

The Nahuas had a polytheistic religion. They questioned the nature of existence, the Divine and the after life. They believed that there is life because of the gods: "Not only did the gods create life at a time 'when there was still darkness' but throughout all time they maintained life" (Leon-Portilla 68). Many early writings focus on the transitoriness of life on earth as well as the illusory nature of life. According to the Nahuatl understanding, nothing endures in this life; thus nothing is true. This conception of life leads to a hedonistic attitude in the Nahua poets as they claim that while living, one must derive the maximum pleasure possible.

In terms of its notion of unification with nature, it may be argued that the Nahuatl religion also has some pantheistic qualities. Despite the polytheistic understanding, "the true god" is the "One" and he is called "the Lord of Duality," Ometeotl. The Nahuatl god is attributed both a masculine and a feminine quality as his equal is a goddess named "the Dual Lady," Omecihuatl.

There are two different Nahuatl myths concerning man's origin in *Historia de Las Mexicanos* and in Fray Gerónimo de Mendieta's record. In both myths, man's creation is attributed to the Lord of Duality with some variations. According to *The Historia* there are four gods, namely Tezcatlipoca, Quetzalcoatl, Huitzilopochtli and Xipe Totec (all representing different aspects of Tezcatlipoca, the son of the Lord of Duality and the Dual Lady), who initially had created fire and the sun, then formed a man and a woman, called Oxomoco and Cipactonal. This man and woman were sent to till the soil. She was asked to spin and weave while they were both commissioned with giving birth to people and with working hard. The following lines, taken from Fray Gerónimo de Mendieta's record, narrate man's creation quite differently:

> They said that when the sun was at nine o'clock, it shot an arrow
> at the mentioned place and a hole was made, from which the first
> man emerged. He had no body from the armpits down, and afterward
> an entire woman emerged from the same place. When they were questioned
> as to how that man without a body had been able to beget, they said
> something foolish and obscene which is not to be recorded here. (87-88)

Based on the translator Angel Maria Garibay's account of Mendiata's gaps, Leon-Portilla states that the untold part implies the man and the woman, both naked, kissed each other and gave birth to a son who became the origin of all mankind (Leon-Portilla 106-107). It may be concluded that women play a significant role in American Indian mythology. Deconstructing the stereotypical associations of Native American women with "squaws" and "princesses," Meldan Tanrısal calls women in Native American myths "corn maidens" since they are both "life-givers" and "sustainers of life," similar to the corn which is assigned a significant role of creation in Indian myths (par. 28). In American Indian mythology, women are depicted as reflections of nature with their power of creation which symbolically involves corn-planting, spinning and weaving.

The Nahuas also believed that human destiny could be predicted through horoscopes. Hence the cycles of the earth and the moon were as crucial as the sun which represents life itself. The Nahuas viewed free will as significant since they thought that every individual can change his own fate to a certain degree. Thus education plays a significant role in the Nahuatl tradition and contributes to a more open and a broader idea of man, by not underestimating the potential of people to make changes in their lives. The Nahuas considered death an awakening from a dream-like existence because, in the Nahuatl understanding, through death they reached "the beyond."(Leon-Portilla 73) The information above also shows that the Nahuas have a symbolic conception of life and death.

The Maya was a Meso-American civilization which was located throughout the southern Mexican states of Chiapas, Tabasco, and the Yucatan Peninsula states of Quintana Roo, Campeche and Yucatán. The Maya area later extended throughout the northern Central American region, including the present-day nations of Guatemala, Belize, El Salvador and western Honduras. The Mayans are noteworthy also for having the only written language of the pre-Columbian Americas, as well as for their art, architecture, and mathematical and astronomical systems. Initially established during the Preclassic period (c. 2000 BC to 250 AD), many Mayan cities reached their highest state of development during the Classic period (c. 250 AD to 900 AD), and continued throughout the Postclassic period until the arrival of the Spanish. The Mayans never disappeared as they survived even after the Spanish colonization of the Americas. Many Mayan languages continue to be spoken as primary languages even today.

Mayan mythology is known to be rich in the representation of sacred animal figures. *Popol Vuh* and *The Rabinal Achi* may be considered the two noteworthy texts of the Mayan Culture. *Popol Vuh* is a text of mytho-history which tells the history of gods and human beings in the Quiche region of today's Guatemala. The text was originally written in hieroglyphics and then in the Roman alphabet (1554-1558). *Popol Vuh* involves different episodes while it provides a record of mankind in two cycles: adventures on earth and the ones in the Mayan underworld, Xibalba. Many critics suggest that *Popul Vuh* requires further consideration as it "survives as a kind of literary hybrid of pre-Hispanic content and colonial form" (Underiner 13).

The Rabinal Achi is the only example of the pre-Hispanic performance text. It is a dance drama from the same region as the *Popol Vuh*. *The Rabinal Achi* deals with a conflict between two Mayan communities as its central issue. A prince from one of the Mayan principalities is the major character in the play. He is captivated while he challenges Rabinal's monopoly on resources in the region. Although owing to his skills as a warrior, the prince is asked to fight for his captor, his patriotism prevails over the offer and finally he chooses death. In this respect the play reflects the irreconcilability of two representatives of local power as well as the significance of cultural codes such as respectability and independence. As Tamara L. Underiner argues, the key theme in *The Rabinal Achi* can be considered "the relationship between cultural identity and geopolitical location" (20). Moreover it may be suggested that cultural identity prevails as the hero is spiritually decolonized by his choice of death. As mentioned above, the Indian and Scottish myths deal with nature as an orderly and unifying force. Both Indian and Scottish myths depict forces of nature work together in harmony. In other words, there is no hierarchy but a cyclic turn between deities as each and every one of them represents a different aspect of nature.

The Mayan myth *Popol Vuh* and the Scottish myth *Beira, Queen of Winter* will be studied as alternative myths of Other cultures. While *Popol Vuh* foregrounds a different creation myth, *Beira*'s stories set forth an alternative to the patriarchal structure in early Greek myths. When the stories of the Olympian deities are considered, the mother goddess Hera is a secondary deity as compared to Zeus, in all aspects. However, Beira is the mother of all Scottish deities and is hardly challenged, even by her strongest son, the Summer King. As for *Popol Vuh,* there is an alternative story of creation which in turn challenges the Western myth of *Genesis*.

Sam Colop's edition of *Popol Vuh* introduces an empty world, very silent and stable. In *Popol Vuh*, the creation of humans is traced to the three feathered serpents living in water, called 'Gucumatz' (serpents are Maya symbols for rebirth and regeneration) and to three other deities, Caculha Huracan, Chipi Caculha and Raxa Cachulca (the three deities are together called Heart of Heaven). When these gods join the serpents in an attempt to create human beings to praise them, their first two attempts fail. As they attempt to make men of mud, men cannot move or speak. The second time they create wooden creatures that can speak but have no soul or blood and quickly forget their creators. According to the most well-known version of the legend, the gods destroy both the mud men and the wooden men. In their final and successful attempt, the flesh of "true people" is made out of white and yellow corn while their arms and legs are made of cornmeal.

This account of man's creation contradicts the traditional account of creation by monotheistic religions. The following quote, taken from Book VII of *Paradise Lost* reflects the argument in *Genesis* and reveals the Western belief concerning man's creation:

> Let us make now Man in our image, Man
> In our similitude, and let them rule
> Over the Fish and Fowle of Sea and Aire,
> Beast of the Field, and over all the Earth,
> And every creeping thing that creeps the ground.
> This said, he formd thee, Adam, thee O Man
> Dust of the ground, and in thy nostrils breath'd
> The breath of Life; in his own Image hee
> Created thee, in the Image of God
> Express, and thou becam'st a living Soul.
> Male he created thee, but thy consort
> Female for Race; then bless'd Mankinde, and said,
> Be fruitful, multiplie, and fill the Earth,
> Subdue it, and throughout Dominion hold
> Over Fish of the Sea, and Fowle of the Aire,
> And every living thing that moves on the Earth.
> Wherever thus created, for no place. (l 519-535)

Popol Vuh's story of creation challenges that of *Paradise Lost* in two respects:

> - Instead of the three creators in *Popol Vuh*, *Paradise Lost* introduces only one.
>
> - The man in *Paradise Lost* is formed out of dust instead of corn. In this respect, the Mayan myth of *Popol Vuh* contradicts the Western myths of Genesis and sets forth an alternative story of creation.

The Scottish myth of *Beira* centralizes a female deity and thereby dethrones the patriarchy in the myth of Olympian gods and goddesses. Beira the Queen of Winter is the mother of all gods and goddesses in Scotland. Everyone fears her because "[w]hen roused to anger she was as fierce as the biting North wind and harsh as the tempest-stricken sea" (MacKenzie 22). Since her power is of more concern, there is no more than a little note about her feminine qualities in Beira's depiction:

> As soon as Beira tested the magic water, in silence and alone,
> She began to grow young again. She left the island and returning
> to Scotland, fell into a magic sleep. When , at length, she awoke,
> in bright sunshine, she rose up as a beautiful girl with long hair
> as buds of broom, cheeks red as rowen berries, and blue eyes that
> sparkled like the summer sea in sunshine. (24)

However her beauty does not last long and she grows old again. Her old age, which is a sign of wisdom, is foregrounded many times in the story. The following lines exemplify how her oldness is centralized:

> O life that ebbs like the sea!
> I am weary and old, I am weary and old-
> Oh! How can I happy be
> All alone in the dark and the cold.
>
> I'm the old Beira again,
> My mantle no longer is green.
> I think of my beauty with pain
> And the days when another was queen.
>
> My arms are withered and thin,
> My hair once golden is grey;
> 'T is winter- my reign doth begin-
> Youth's summer has faded away.
>
> Youth's summer and autumn have fled-
> I am weary and old, I am weary and old.
> Every flower must fade and fall dead
> When the winds blow cold, when the winds blow cold. (25)

Beira is not praised for her beauty which is quite unconventional. Moreover, the Scottish myths depict Beira as a figure of authority. Beira has a significant power even over other deities. In one of the myths, she keeps Bride as a prisoner because Beira's fairest son Angus-the-Ever-Young (the Summer King) has fallen in love with Bride. When the two lovers get married against her will, Beira is in such a fury that "[a]ll the fairies fled in terror into the mound and all the doors were shut" (MacKenzie 42).

All these aspects of Beira are very different from those of the Olympian goddess Hera. Unlike Beira, Hera is always praised for her golden hair which is a sign of her beauty. Furthermore, Hera is secondary to Zeus who asserts his omnipotence in the following lines:

> Nothing can be revoked or said in vain
> nor unfulfilled if I should nod my head. (Homer L 526-527)

However Beira is depicted as the most powerful one among both male and female deities. She is commonly praised for her wisdom which conventionally is a male quality. In this respect, Beira might be likened to the Olympian goddess Athena. However, the Greek myths often depict the Olympian goddess Athena as half female and half male so as to account for her so-called male qualities. On the other hand Beira is not a peaceful character like Athena since she frequently challenges the authority of other gods and goddesses. Nature has a significant role in both Indian and Scottish mythology. Unlike Greek and Roman myths which involve cultural connotations such as rivalry and hierarchy, in other words, power struggle, Indian and Scottish myths deal with balance, harmony and temporariness in nature. As Beira's reign always ends when winter is over and the Dual Lord and Lady are given equal power, these myths imply reconciliation instead of oppression.

The Mayan myth of *Popul Vuh* and the Scottish myth of *Beira* both tell the two universal stories of mankind, namely creation and the cycle of the year, from their own traditional perspectives. While *Popul Vuh* sets forth a story of creation out of corn, *Beira* centralizes female power in nature. In this respect, both myths provide alternative stories on the generation of mankind as well as the order of nature.

In other words, the two myths introduce other possible truths to be studied, and hence challenge the conventionally studied myths. This idea is reinforced by the following arguments of some major postcolonial critics. In his introduction to *Scottish Wonder Tales From Myth and Legend*, Donald A. MacKenzie notes that the Scottish deities have never been popularized like those of ancient Greece (21). Similarly, Gloria Anzaldua complains about the ignorance and indifference toward the indigenous roots of the Chicana/o culture (228, 234-235) and calls for a spiritual migration to their Indian roots, in her own words "the return odyssey to the historical/mythological Aztlan" (33).

The fact that mainstream Western literature has always been on the agenda has inevitably led to an oppression of its Other, namely the so called Third World Literatures. With the rising interest in postcolonial studies, writings of the Other ethnic-origined cultures are finally being included in the literature course syllabi.

This scrutiny of Other literatures has paved the way for a revisitation of oriental myths as well.

4.2. Notes on the Scottish and Chicano/a Traditions of Writing

Scottish literature may be defined as literature written in Scotland or by Scottish authors. Scottish literature dates back to the sixth century and most of the literature composed then is in Brythonic (old Welsh), Gaelic, Latin or Old English languages. The first known text to be composed in the form of early Scots is *Brus,* which appeared in the fourteenth century. Its writer, John Barbour— contemporary to Geoffrey Chaucer—is often called the father of Scots poetry.

In the late Medieval period, the Brus, which combines historical romance with verse chronicle, was celebrated as the most popular poetic genre in Scotland. Influenced by Classical, French and Chaucerian literary languages, Scots poetry welcomed different genres of literature during the fifteenth century. The late fifteenth and mid-sixteenth centuries are considered to be a golden age in Scottish literature. Walter Kennedy, Robert Henryson, William Dunbar, Gavin Douglas and David Lyndsay are among the noteworthy writers of the period. David Lyndsay's *Ane Pleasant Satyre of the Thrie Estaitis* is a significant example of the earliest dramatic tradition in Scots literature.

Seventeenth century introduced prominent figures of Scottish literature such as Robert Sempil, Lady Wardlaw and Lady Grizel Baillie. The Scottish novel, among the pioneers of which one can note Tobias Smollett, started during the eighteenth century. Robert Burns and Walter Scott can be considered the two major representatives of the Romantic Movement in Scottish literature. While Burns is often called the national bard of Scottish culture, Scott, whose *Waverley* is the first historical novel, is considered a patriot. James Hogg, whose work revisited the Scottish religious tradition, can be noted among the major writers inspired by Scott.

The patriotic stance in Scottish literature started especially after the 1850s when a yearning for a rural Scottish life started. The Scottish landscape has been a great tool for Scottish literature ever since. The late nineteenth century was a witness to a taste for adventure novels and science fiction in Scotland. Sir Canon Doyle's *Sherlock Holmes* and Robert Louis Stevenson's *Treasure Island, Strange Case of Dr. Jekyll and Mr Hyde* are among the noteworthy works of the genre.

The early twentieth century was witness to the rise in the use of Lowlands Scots while there were also a remarkable number of writings in standard English. One can recall Hugh MacDiarmid, Eric Linklater, A.J. Cronin, Naomi Mitchison, Douglas Young, Robert Garioch, James Bridie, Robert McLellan, Nan Shepherd, William Soutar and Sidney Goodsir Smith.

Contemporary Scottish writing is reflective of the absence of a specific national literary stance as A.L. Kennedy notes: "the cultural history of Scotland has been a lot about having no identity" (qtd. in March 102-103). Significant figures of Scottish writing, such as James Kennaway, Edwin Morgan, Alasdair Gray, James Kelman, Irvine Welsh, Ian Rankin, Ian Banks, Alan Warner, Muriel Spark and Alexander McCall Smith are among the canonical figures of contemporary literature. While subject matter varies, there is a revival in fantastic fiction as well as a specific interest in writing about rural versus urban Scotland. A.L.Kennedy (a Scottish writer of novels, short stories and non-fiction), Janice Galloway (a Scottish writer of novels, short stories, prose-poetry and non-fiction), Ali Smith (A Scottish writer of novels, short stories and a play), Leaila Aboulela (An Arabic Scottish writer of novels and short stories) and Jackie Kay (a black Scottish lesbian novelist and poet) can be considered among the noteworthy women writers, making a call for a strong female canon in Scottish literature. The latter two commonly write about ethnic and gender identity as well as the dual or in-between states. Carol Ann Duffy, the first openly queer female poet in Scottish literature, is their counterpart in poetry. Duffy's poetry deals with women's oppression and lesbian identity. Duffy's following poem, 'Anne Hathaway' a poem written for Shakespeare's wife and published in the collection entitled *World Wives*, is a critical exploration of women's emotionally oppressed situation in marriage:

> *'Item I gyve unto my wife my second best bed ...'*
> (from Shakespeare's will)
>
> The bed we loved in was a spinning world
> of forests, castles, torchlight, clifftops, seas
> where we would dive for pearls. My lover's words
> were shooting stars which fell to earth as kisses
> on these lips; my body now a softer rhyme
> to his, now echo, assonance; his touch
> a verb dancing in the centre of a noun.
> Some nights, I dreamed he'd written me, the bed

> a page beneath his writer's hands. Romance
> and drama played by touch, by scent, by taste.
> In the other bed, the best, our guests dozed on,
> dribbling their prose. My living laughing love—
> I hold him in the casket of my widow's head
> as he held me upon that next best bed.

The poem reveals the binary oppositions between women and men, respectively as private versus public and sentimental versus realist which, according to feminist thought, are reinforced by marriage, an institution serving patriarchy. Duffy's poem is in dialogue with Shakespeare's will, but foregrounds Hathaway's gaze in their marriage bed while it decentralizes Shakespeare's male gaze.

As theatre is a well recognized ground for social protest, it is mostly through the Scottish Theatre that a specific patriotic trend is being hosted. Its nationalist stance reinforces a literary quest to re-explore the Scottish authentic ties and formulate its own national perspective. Harrower and Greig, two remarkable Scottish dramatists, set this fact forth:

> To redefine ourselves we need to understand ourselves, exchange ideas
> and aspirations, confront enduring myths, expose injustices, and explore
> our past. The quality, accessibility, and immediacy of Scottish theatre make
> it one of the best arenas in which these dialogues can take place.
> (Holdsworth and Luckhurst 126)

As Holdsworth and Luckhurst note, the Scottish playwrights have dealt with "evoking" particular places and landscapes in Scotland, especially the ones that exist on the border of the nation, in their searches for their past and present national identities as well as their personal ones (126). To Holdsworth and Luckhurst, the highlands and the islands of Scotland, which are considered "barbarian, backward and savage," are the most noteworthy places signifying both "remote[ness]" and "isolation," in turn the "real Scotland" (126-127). While the topographical understanding of the Scottish border (to England) implies the land between the River Tweed on the east coast and the Solway Firth in the west, it metaphorically connotes the in-between state of identities as symbolized by the Highlands (the mountainous part of the land) and the islands versus the Lowlands (the central valley). The metaphorical understanding of "border," a term which the Chicana theorist Gloria Anzaldua calls "a dividing line" meant to "distinguish *us* from *them*" (25) has been a significant tool for Scottish writing as well. While the Scottish dramatists employ many different themes in their plays, they have a common interest in representing ethnic and gender issues on the stage. Among the pioneers of contemporary Scottish drama, one can recall David Greig, David Harrower, Zinnie Harris, Sue Glover, Rona Munro, Chris Hannan, Alison Smith and Liz Lochhead make great contributions toward the canonization of their literatures.

A similar effort toward canonization is currently reflected in Chicano writing Chicano literature can be defined as the literature written by Mexican Americans (Chicanos/Chicanas) living in the United States. Historians suggest that the early roots of Chicano literature date back to the sixteenth century, when the Spanish adventurer Cabeza de Vaca published an account of his experience with indigenous groups in southwest America. Besides the writings of Spanish adventurers, Indian oral literature has significantly contributed to Chicano literature. Most of Chicano literature was composed during and after the mid-19th century as an outcome of the Mexican-American war and the USA's invasion of half of the Mexican land. The Mexicans who then became American citizens are called Chicano/(a)s. Reinforcing the Chicano movement which is a social protest claiming that Chicanos cannot freely represent themselves, Chicano literature deals specifically with themes of ethnic oppression, discriminaton, border culture; and broadly with identity, culture, migration. Their writing directly reflects the in-between (as both Mexican and American) and bilingual (English and Spanish-speaking) identities of Chicana/os. The following lines by Elba Rosario Sanchez set forth the dual experience of Chicanas:

> Two years after moving to the United States, right before my fourteenth birthday, mi mami and papi planned our first return visit to Mexico. I didn't know then just how revealing this trip would be for me. Only later did I realize that this was to be a painful journey into questioning myself, that I would be forced to look at myself through my own Mexican family's eyes. Before, my identity was questioned by an outsider, someone not from within mi cultura, ahora seria diferente. (35)

The involvement of Spanish words in English sentences, implies that English alone fails to account for the Chicana/o experience. The recurrent Spanish intrusion , especially in reference to "significant others" such as mother, father and culture, may be linked to Sanchez's search to view herself through her Mexican ties. In this respect , Sanchez's lines are quite reminiscient of the black theorist Du Bois's following consideration of the negro experience: "....this sense of looking at oneself through the eyes of the other." (2) An "outsider" to herself, Sanchez speaks through what Du Bois calls "double consciousness." (2) In other words, the American self of Sanchez or her internalized Otherness had been questioning her Mexican self.

Chicano(a) writing broadly addresses the above-mentioned theme of identity conflict. Among the major writers of Chicano literature are Americo Paredes, Sandra Cisneros, Rudolfo Anaya, Rudolfo Acuna, Rudolfo Gonzales, Gary Soto, John Rechy, Oscar Zeta Acosta, Luis Omar Salinas, Alicia Gaspar de Alba, Maria Ruiz de Burton, Benjamin Alire Saenz, Felipe de Ortego y Gasca and Ana Castillo.

As for drama, Luis Valdez, who is also the founder of El Teatro Campesino, is one of the most prominent playwrights of Chicano literature. Representing the ethnic oppression the Chicano are exposed to, in his play *Zoot Suit* among others, Valdez initiated the tradition of indigenism in Chicana/o Theatre. However Chicana playwrights (among the pioneers one can note Denise Chavez, Evalina Fernandez, Josefina Lopez and Cherrie L. Moraga) are quite at odds with Valdez. Cherrie L.Moraga relates this situation to their male counterpart's limited representation of women characters. (142)

In her theoretical work entitled *Borderlands,* the Chicana lesbian feminist critic Gloria Anzaldua defines the location of the Chicanas as on the "borderland" which she calls "a vague and undetermined place created by the emotional residue of an unnatural boundary" (25)/ To Anzaldua, the experience there may be considered "a constant state of transition" and its inhabitants "prohibited and forbidden", "los atravesados" (5). In other words they are the Others from the Gringo's perspective. In *Borderlands*, Anzaldua also makes a call for reclaiming Aztlan,the original land of the Indian Americans (23-35). Anzaldua's suggestion of *border crossing* which metaphorically indicates a re-exploration of the Chicana identity, received a positive response from Chicana playwrights.

4.3. Cherrie Moraga and Liz Lochhead's Drama in their National Canons

The Scottish feminist playwright Liz Lochhead and the Chicana lesbian dramatist Cherrie L. Moraga contribute to their own national traditions by revisiting ethnic myths with a critical perspective on race and gender issues. Moraga and Lochhead not only explore their ethnic roots by retracing Indian and Celtic myths, but also combine them with some major Greek and Roman myths. In this respect they challenge the hegemony of Western myths by bringing into them alternative contexts. Moraga's and Lochhead's authentic rewritings of some Greek and Roman myths in postcolonial and feminist contexts will be studied in the following two chapters.

Liz Lochhead (born in 1947) is one of the most popular playwrights and poets of Scotland. She studied at Glasgow School of Art where she later taught fine arts until becoming a professional writer. Currently she is teaching at Glasgow University. Her plays include *Blood and Ice*, *Mary Queen of Scots Got Her Head Chopped Off* (1987) and *Perfect Days* (2000). Lochhead's poetry collections include *True Confessions and New Clichés* (1985), *Bagpipe Muzak* (1991) and *Dreaming Frankenstein: and Collected Poems* (1984). Her adaptation of Molière's *Tartuffe* (1985) into Scots was well received by the audience. In 2001 she won the Saltire Society Scottish Book of the Year Award with her adaptation of Euripides' *Medea*. Her most recent rewriting (2003) is Sophocles' *Thebans*.

The Scottish playwright Liz Lochhead takes feminist and postcolonial perspectives in her plays. Lochhead has three published original plays, namely *Blood and Ice*, *Mary The Queen of Scotts Got Her Head Chopped Off* and *Perfect Days*, besides her several adaptations of classics into Scots which will be examined in the following two chapters. Lochhead's plays deal with gender roles and stereotypes and in specific with women's oppression. Since most of her plays address gender issues, Lochhead's patriotic stance may be considered secondary to to her feminist consciousness. However, Lochhead's plays also introduce the reader to a Scottish context which is usually reinforced by Lochhead's use of Scottish diction.

Blood and Ice is an innovative play telling the story of *Frankenstein*'s creation by Mary Shelley. The play starts with a scene in a house party in which young Mary Shelley, her husband Percy B. Shelley, her half-sister Claire and Lord Byron make a bet on who can write the scariest story. The play reflects the process by which Mary Shelley becomes a highly reputed novelist of the Gothic genre. Lochhead's play effectively shows parallelisms between the pathetic sides of Lochhead's own life story and those of the monster in *Frankenstein* through juxtapositions and flashbacks. Revisiting the myth of *Frankenstein*, Lochhead deals with the questions of mankind's violation of nature for our own hedonic pleasures as well as man's 'oppression of' and/or 'by' its Other. In her Introduction to the play, Lochhead suggests that the myth Mary Shelley introduced is transformed and will even "remain potent for our nuclear age, our age of astonishment and unease at the fruits of perhaps-beyond-the-boundaries of genetic experimentation." [quotation missing]

Mary Queen of Scots Got Her Head Chopped Off deals with the relationship between Elizabeth 1 and Mary Stuart in a postcolonial and feminist context. The play's focus on the Scottish Queen, Mary, textually decentralizes the English Queen, Elizabeth 1. In addition the play introduces the Scottish Queen as an unconventional female figure by foregrounding her love affair with Bothwell while she tries to find ways to divorce Lord Darnley. The following quote from the play reflects not only Mary's adultery but also her reluctance to care for her dying husband:

> (Mary and Bothwell kiss and sink down to the floor in love-making rolling over and over. Drums are building on a crescendo. Darnley where she left him on the sickbed, murmurs her name.)
> Justice!
> (And at this time, the very word makes an enormous explosion happen as Darnley at Kirk O'Field goes up. As smoke clears everyone else but Mary and Bothwell, who are still writhing in love-making on the floor, begins an accusatory chant.)
> All: Burn the hoor! Burn the hoor! (Lochhead 1989:60)

The use of the word "hoor," which is the Scottish version of the word "whore," functions not only as an indicator of the Scottish diction but also as a sign of the common perspective directed toward Mary, as the Other of conventions. The play depicts two strong women, Mary and Elizabeth, as Others of each other: Scotland versus England, Catholicism versus Anglicanism, extramarital sexuality versus virginity. However they are both represented as two strong female protagonists, both in search of power and authority, in a patriarchal society. In Carla Rodriguez Gonzalez's interview, Lochhead notes that the play deals not only with Scotland and England, male and female, Catholicism and Protestanism but also with "civil power" and "some sort of democracy growing..." (2004:105). In this respect, the play has to do with binary opposites as it finally challenges them by offering an image of children at the end. Lochhead views the function of children in the play as very significant since it enables the play to pose the question, "'Do we have to always be like this?'" as opposed to the statement already made: "'This is who we are'" (105). In other words, the play makes a serious effort to destabilize the conventional notion of self and Other, which serves its feminist and postcolonial purposes. One can consider La Corbie, who announces to the audience that she is telling her own version of the story, as a sign of the postcolonial discourse embedded in the play. It is through the narration of the fantastic creature La Corbie, presented as a bird-woman, that previous historical narrations of the period are challenged. Given this context, La Corbie signifies the dilemma between fantasy and reality or story and history. In her interview with Lochhead, Gonzalez suggests that La Corbie who stands for "the spirit of Scotland" as an "ambiguous creature," "invites us not to trust official discourse, not even official subversive discourse" (104). In this respect the play takes a New Historicist perspective, the central conflict of which is called by Stanley Fish " the problem of reconciling the assertion of 'wall to wall' textuality—the denial that the writing of history could find its foundation in a substratum of an unmediated fact—with the desire to say something specific and normative" (303).

In *Perfect Days*, Lochhead has no postcolonial concern although she employs a distinctly Scottish diction as in her other plays. In *Perfect Days,* the protagonist is Barbs Marshall who is a successful woman in the beauty business. Getting close to her fortieth birthday, she decides to have a baby. Her excessive attachment to her mother may be a major factor in the postponing of her own maternity. Lochhead foregrounds gender roles and stereotypes as instruments serving the patriarchy's oppression of women while she challenges them through her unconventional female protagonist, Barbs. Juxtaposing Barbs's friend Alice's conventional life (married, with two children) with that of Barbs, Lochhead asserts Barbs's difference. Lochhead also leaves room for women's oppression by men with references to Barbs's husband, David, who impregnated a young girl. As Barbs looks for sperm, the play gradually asserts its feminist discourse. The female body and its right for maternity are announced while the female-male intercourse and paternity are reduced to sperm.

Another challenging figure in contemporary feminist drama, Cherrie L. Moraga (born in 1952), is a well-known Chicana lesbian playwright. She holds an MA in English from San Francisco State University. Moraga has taught drama and writing in various universities in the States. She is currently an artist in residence at Stanford University. Moraga received several awards for her plays. Yet she is better known for *This Bridge Called My Back: Writings by Radical Women of Color*, an anthology of Chicana feminist thought, co-edited with Gloria Anzaldua. Dealing with both race and feminism, writings in this anthology laid the foundation for third wave feminism in the USA. Moraga's works include *Watsonville: Some Place Not Here; Circle in the Dirt* (2002), *The Hungry Woman* (2001), *Waiting in the Wings: Portrait of a Queer Motherhood* (1997), *Heroes and Saints and Other Plays* (1994), T*he Last Generation: Prose and Poetry* (1993), *The Sexuality of Latinas* (co-editor, 1993), *Shadow of a Man* (1992), *Giving Up the Ghost: Teatro in Two Acts* (1986), *Cuentos: Stories By Latinas* (co-editor, 1983), *Loving in the War Years: Lo que nunca pasó por sus labios* (1983), *This Bridge Called My Back* (co-editor, 1981). Her *The Hungry Woman* involves two of her adaptations; *The Hungry Woman* (*A Mexican Medea*) and *Heart of The Earth* (An adaptation of *Popul Vuh*).

Cherrie Moraga's plays commonly deal with the situation of Chicanas in the States while exploring their lives, relationships and traditions. The life-long oppression Chicanas are exposed to within their patriarchal culture and outside as Others of white Caucasian power structures, may broadly account for the recurrent themes in Moraga's plays. Moraga's first collection of plays, *Heroes and Saints and Other Plays* (1994), includes three plays, "Giving Up the Ghost," "Shadow of a Man" and "Heroes and Saints," respectively. "Giving Up the Ghost", a play in three acts, introduces Marisa (a Chicana in her late 20s), Corky (Marisa as a teenager) and Amalia (a Mexican-born woman, a generation older than Marisa). The play is a collection of Marisa's irreconcilable memories of childhood as Corky and later those of desire for another woman, Amalia. The play deals with Marisa's search for a way to unite the different segments of her identities as a Chicana, woman and queer while at the same time presenting a passionate love story between two women— one being a lesbian, Marisa, the other a heterosexual, Amalia. The play's bilingualism and its incorporation of indigenous settings and music on the background display a specifically Chicana/o context. The male exploration of the female body (Alejandro's touching of Amalia)is associated with the invasion of the Mexican land by the Americans. Hence Amalia dreams that she and Marisa are in a Mexican desert, thinking that they might have a chance to be together there. The critic Yvonne Yarbro-Bejarano traces the function of Mexico in the play to "a femininized place" which "does not simply refer to nationhood or ethnicity" but rather to "a mythic place of origins, authenticity, wholeness" (39, 40). In this respect Marisa's desire for Amanda may be related to her wish to unite with her Other half; a yearning to meet her indigenous roots. In the following lines; Amanda states that Marisa projects her curiosity of Mexico onto everything: "Her nostalgia for the land she had never seen was everywhere: in her face, her drawings, her love of the hottest sand by the sea" (17). That her lines are followed by their first kiss, accompanied by "indigenous flutes and drums" (17) reinforces the idea that Amanda might function as an extension or a reflection of Marisa's desire for her indigenous ties. In this respect, their queer identities are moved onto an indigenous context which is directly reinforced by the Chicana feminist theorists's interpretation of Anzaldua's conception of Chicana body, *bocacalles*, as "an intersection where two streets cross one another" (2). Similarly, Anzaldua's suggestion of Aztlan—the mythical land of the Aztecs—as a home for the Other, *los atravesados*, involving the queer, situates the queer issue on an archaic ground (24-35). Such a collective treatment of the queer issue as well as the engendered context of the Mexican land, produces in the play an authentic dialogue with contemporary postcolonial and feminist discourses. The device also contributes to its positive reception by its audience whom the play involves in its list of characters as "People." Moraga's two-act play "Shadow of a Man" deals with the family secrets of the Rodriguez (an extended family including two daughters, Leticia and Lupe, a son, Rigo, and the aunt, Rosario, as well as the parents, Manuel and Hortensia Rodriguez)—especially the parents' hidden sexual desire for Manuel's best friend, Conrado. The shadow of Conrado has always been with the family not only because Manuel always recalls him as his male role model but also because Conrado had spent one night with Hortensia and is the biological father of Lupe. The most pathetic side of the play is Manuel's offering his wife to his *compadre*, Conrado, for one night, thirteen years ago. For all these years, he has been very jealous of Hortensia not because his wife slept with another man but because she got closer to Conrado than he could ever get. Hortensia also lives in Conrado's shadow as she feels a strong sense of guilt. When years later the family is visited by Conrado, Manuel witnesses the revival of emotions between Hortensia and Conrado. Manuel's obsession with Conrado then leads to a big disappointment and Manuel finally commits suicide. Moraga notes that the play was inspired by a "fascination with how Latino men value each other so much, in the face of that, women are sort of like functionaries, objects in the dealing of men's relationships with themselves" (Lovato 24). Moraga's play highlights the public nature of the female body within the patriarchy by displaying its victimization by Chicano *machismo*. The play's colored feminist stance is also asserted by the presence of a dark feminist character, Leticia, who challenges not only the submission of the colored,

> Leticia (exciting): 'Bout the time you're in college, lots of Chicanos will be going to Harvard. You'll see. (72)

but also patriarchy's oppression of women and women's internalized Otherness:

> Hortensia: [...] That's what you want, isn't it? To be free like a man.
> Leticia: That wouldn't be so bad.
> Hortensia: [...] If God had wanted you to be a man, he would of given you something between your legs.
> Leticia: I have something between my legs. (76, 77)

The last lines quoted above echo the perspective of Luce Irigaray whose suggestion of *ecriture feminine* deconstructs all phallogocentric perspectives which define women through the lackor absence of a phallus by calling them "hysteria scenario" (60). The play's unconventional stance is also supported by the characterization of Lupe who initially questions the norms: "How do you really know what's regular life and what's a sueno?" (53), and later discards heterosexuality. As Yarbro-Bejarano suggests, the play owes its success to its "interrogation of the cultural construction of gender roles and the creation of a space within Chicano culture for the recognition of diverse and fluid sexual identities." (63)

"Heroes and Saints" is a play in two acts which focuses on the pesticide that poisons the people of McLaughin (a fictive place) and leads to cancer, birth defects and death. The author's notes for the play state that she was inspired by the cancer cluster in McFarland, a town in the San Joaquin Valley in California, in the 1980s (89). It is common knowledge that most of the inhabitants of the valley are Chicanos and Moraga's play relates the uncontrolled use of chemicals and pesticides in places where indigenous people live, to environmental racism. Moraga employs fantastic elements and mythical references as well as historical events in the play which contextually serve her postcolonial purpose. For instance the character Cerezita is represented as a head only, without a body, as she was born that way because of the pesticides. Cerezita's mother, Dolores, represents a stereotypical woman and mother figure since her perspective on the female gender, displays an internalized patriarchy: "Why you wannu make yourself como una mujer? [like a woman] [...]

God made you a man and you throw it away. You lower yourself into half a man" (123, 124). The above quote in which Dolores addresses her homosexual son, Mario, echoes the conventional and male-centered conception of women as half a man. The two characters Cerezita and Father Juan, two virgins who fall in love with each other, are reminiscient of the myth of the Virgin of Guadalupe. Most Catholics believe that in the sixteenth century, a young indigenous boy named Juan (who was called Saint Juan Diego after this incident) saw the apparition of theVirgin Mary as the Virgin of Guadalupe while he was walking toward his village in Mexico City. According to the legend, Juan Diego saw a vision of a young girl who spoke in the local language of Nahuatl and was surrounded by light. The Lady asked for a church to be built in her honor. Juan Diego recognized her as the Virgin Mary and told the entire story to the Spanish bishop. The bishop wanted Juan Diego to ask for a miracle so that they could make sure that she is the Virgin Mary. The Lady sent Juan Diego to gather some flowers from the top of Tepeyac Hill (where Juan Diego saw the Lady's apparition) although there were no flowers around as it was winter time. Juan Diego gathered some Castilian roses which the Virgin rearranged in Juan's *tilma* (blanket, cape). When Juan Diego presented the roses to the bishop, the image of the Virgin of Guadalupe appeared imprinted on the cloth of Diego's tilma, as one of her miracles. This reference is further supported as Cerezita and her wheelchair finally change into an altar, involving the figure of theVirgin of Guadalupe. The play's involvement of these legendary figures reinforces its feminist and postcolonial discourses. The virgin aspect of the female body is revisited especially by the radical feminists, as a sign of the lesbian love which is idealized in two virgin bodies, virgin for ever. Reference to the Virgin of Guadalupe reveals an indigenous context not only because the apparition took place in Mexico but also because the lady spoke in the local Indian language. The play also involves real, historical events, especially through its recurrent references to the political activist, Cezar Chavez. Chavez is the founder of both the National Farm Workers Association (NFWA) and the United Farm Workers (UFW). Chavez is better known for his five-year boycott of the California grape growers, and protest against the use of pesticides harmful to farm workers and the poor working conditions of workers. By incorporating reality and fantasy, history and myths or legends, the play challenges hegemonies of power and discourse, in adherence to a Foucaultian understanding of history in terms of "dominance" and "shifting power relations" (Foucault 1980: 154).

Watsonville: Some Place Not Here and *Circle in the Dirt: El Pueblo de East Palo Alto*, two local plays which are published in the same collection, commonly introduce the California of the 1990s, dealing with the white English hegemony oppressing the farm towns and indigenous communities of the state. The plays involve interviews conducted with residents of Watsonville and East Palo Alto, the two towns in the San Francisco Bay Area which neighbor the University of California at Santa Cruz and Stanford University respectively. The plays relate the new cultural identity reinforced by university life to the legitimization of the so-called "First World Power." In her foreword to the plays, Moraga notes that these two Californian towns are specifically chosen, because

> East Palo Alto and Watsonville are prototypes of what is lost and found in the natural and peopled beauty of the state: the living memory of pre-conquest paradise in the coastal and bay shore landscapes today; the horror of state-sanctioned racism made manifest in drug-related gang violence and immigrant rights abuse. Each town also boasts a history, which has resisted Corporate America (and continues to do so) as long and as hard as possible. (viii)

The plays reflect an indigenous stance, reinforcing what is called the salad-bowl image of the States, as opposed to that of the melting pot. In other words, both plays broadly address the issue of white Caucasian power versus poor, colored communities. Moraga reflects her feminist and postcolonial objectives once again as her drama gathers the two communities in a challenge to cultural and economic oppression. The following quote from Susana in *Watsonville*, directly poses the central question of both plays: "Where is home for the dispossessed Chicanada?" (44) to which this conversation of Chuy and Professor in *Circle in the Dirt*, may be considered an answer:

> Chuy: ...What chu gonna do Profe, after they tear up this field?
> Professor: Find another piece of dirt, I guess. Black people, people of color in general, we are an earth people. [...] We belong to the earth. (139)

Liz Lochhead and Cherrie Moraga share a common ground as two successful women playwrights dealing with gender and ethnic issues. In all her original plays, Lochhead owns a distinctly feminist discourse, focusing on gender roles and stereotypes. Lochhead's female protagonists explore their female bodies while they simultaneously search for their identities outside the gendered patterns of their conventional societies. As they suffer from gender oppression, their motivations for challenge are similar to those of Moraga's heroines. Both playwrights draw upon female experiences of body and identity as they celebrate women's physical and spiritual liberty. However unlike Moraga's heroines, Lochhead's female characters explore their bodies through heterosexual relations. Moraga's lesbian feminist stance reflects a more radical but at the same time a stronger criticism of patriarchy and its institutions.

On the other hand, Moraga's postcolonial concerns might be considered as primary as her feminist stance whereas Lochhead's feminism prevails over her Scottish context. While Lochhead foregrounds a Scottish context by using Scottish English and Scottish characters, *Mary Queen of Scots Got Her Head Chopped Off* is her only play—except for the adaptations— involving direct postcolonial discourse. Besides, Lochhead directs a social social criticism toward gender and ethnic oppression, while Moraga's criticism, owing to her background as a theorist, has a more political bent.

In their rewritings of early Greek and Roman myths, both playwrights display their challenges to ethnic and gender oppression more directly. Lochhead and Moraga break the conventional rules of theatre which date back to Aristotle. As mentioned in Chapter 3, the Brazilian critic Augusto Boal argues that the Aristotelian tradition of theatre reinforces oppressive codes and structures. In this respect, both Lochhead's and Moraga's theatre adhere to the Brazilian critic Augusto Boal's challenge to the theatre of the oppressed. Lochhead's and Moraga's authentic insights on rewriting myths of oppression will be discussed in the following two chapters from a comparative and contrastive perspective.

5. Rewriting Myths of Hierarchical and Colonial Oppression

5.1. Liz Lochhead's Scottish Patriotism in *Medea* and *Thebans*

The story in Euripides' play *Medea*, which dates back to 431 B.C., has been retold many times in different ages and multiple contexts. Among the noteworthy adaptations and rewritings of *Medea* in contemporary times, one can recall the Irish playwright Marina Carr's *By the Bog of Cats* which is a modern retelling of *Medea*, Steve Carter's *Pecong* which retells *Medea* in a Caribbean background, the Latina playwright Caridad Svich's *Wreckage* which is a retelling of *Medea* from the two sons' perspectives, Neil Labute's *Medea Redux* and Christa Wolfe's modernized version of *Medea*, as well as Liz Lochhead's and Cherrie L. Moraga's rewritings of the play in postcolonial and feminist contexts.

The Scottish playwright Liz Lochhead's version is considered among the most noteworthy rewritings of the play and was awarded the 2001 Saltire Scottish Book of the Year. Lochhead's play adheres to Euripides' *Medea* with its plot and characterization. Both plays follow a linear plot and have most of the characters such as Medea, Nurse, Jason, Kreon, Glauke and the sons in common. However Lochhead's play introduces a postcolonial perspective, revisiting M*edea* in a distinctly Scottish context. Lochhead's play announces its Scottish background even at the very beginning, in the first stage directions: "*The people of this country all have Scots accents, their language varies from Scots to Scots-English- from time to time and from character to character—and the particular emotional state of the character*" (3). Moreover, Lochhead's version reflects an alternative stance as it restates the very first stage direction of the original play: "[Enter from the house Medea's nurse]" (Euripides 9) as "*A woman is talking to herself and us. This is the NURSE*" (3). It may be observed that the Nurse whom Euripides' play defines in relation to Medea, as her object, is made a subject and given a voice in Lochhead's version. The capitalization of the letters of the word 'NURSE' also implies a foregrounding of the Nurse, which is further asserted as Lochhead introduces a questioning NURSE ;

> I wish to all the Gods it had never sailed the Argo
> had never set its proud prow atween the humped blue rocks
> of distant islands forced itsel through straits
> breisted waves to the land on unlucky Kolchis why?
> why did the sun ever heat up the soil
> in which there split that seed
> that sproutit from sapling to a tall tree of girth enough
> to be felled to build its keel? why was it ever oared?
> why crewed wi heroes fit to filch the Golden Fleece?
> adventurers!
> my lady Medea would never then have sailed wi Jason
> daft for him doted! (3)

instead of a conformist one:

> How I wish the Argo had never reached the land
> Of Colchis, skimming through the blue Symplegades,
> Nor ever had fallen in the glades of Pelion
> The smitten fir-tree to furnish oars for the hands
> Of heroes who in Pelias's name attempted
> The Golden Fleece! For then my mistress Medea
> Would not have sailed for the towers of the land of Iolcus,
> Her heart on fire with passionate love for Jason. (Euripides, Vellacott translation 9)

The above lines indicate that Euripides' Nurse is depicted as an obedient character who never questions why things are the way they are. Her passive tone is reflected in the first line above: "How I wish,", which reflects her sense of helplessness. Since she is oppressed as a slave, she has no subjective voice in narrating the account of incidents. In all aspects, Euripides' Nurse is destined to be a by-stander, once more reminiscient of her depiction in Euripides' above-mentioned stage directions. However, Lochhead's NURSE who speaks in a distinctly Scottish accent, has a rebellious and subjective tone in her narration. Unlike Euripides' Nurse who modestly conforms to the wishes of the Olympian gods, Lochhead's NURSE continuously poses the question "Why?. Moreover Lochhead's NURSE freely comments on characters and incidents. For instance she includes personal remarks as she refers to the prow of the ship Argo as "proud" and calls the heroes after the Golden Fleece "adventurers" (3).

Furthermore, Lochhead's NURSE owns a distancing perspective to Medea:

> I'm feart for her fear her
> I shut my eyes and see Medea

> creepan trough the labyrinthine palace
> follying her hatred like a thread
> I dream of a dagger thrust in yon double bed
> skewering the lovers thegither
> I see the skailt blood of Kreon the king
> she's capable of onything. (4)

The first two lines indicate that the NURSE is not only anxious for Medea but also afraid of Medea. The NURSE's description of Medea's movements in the palace involves an observer's distance as she visualizes Medea "creeping" through the labyrinth-like palace. Moreover, her last line announces a serious sense of fear as the NURSE notes that she expects "anything" from Medea. It may be suggested that Lochhead's NURSE views Medea as her Other which is quite unlike Euripides' Nurse's perspective toward Medea as her alter-ego:

> I am afraid she may think of some dreadful thing,
> For her heart is violent. She will never put up with
> The treatment she is getting. I know and fear her
> Lest she may sharpen a sword and thrust to the heart,
> Stealing into the palace where the bed is made,
> Or even kill the king and the new-wedded groom,
> And thus bring a greater misfortune on herself. (Euripides 10)

As the above lines indicate, in the original version, the Nurse feels a great empathy for Medea whom she knows "well." The Nurse's lines announce that she is afraid Medea may commit suicide, while she is also scared of Medea killing Jason and the King. However the last line makes clear that Euripides' Nurse has serious concern for what Medea's situation will be after the murder rather than for the act of murder itself.

The Scottish perspective of Lochead's NURSE also confirms her status as an outsider in the land. Through her, Lochhead has easy access to the Scottish context of her play. For instance, the NURSE's account of the incidents relates to "distant islands" the Greek city states, each and every one of which Euripides patriotically names (3). From the Scottish NURSE's perspective, the cycle of nature becomes more emphasized. The following lines of the NURSE which are repeated at the end of the play, refer to the ancient Scottish belief system which relates daily events to the cycle of nature, as mentioned in Chapter 4:

> why did the sun ever heat up the soil
> in which there split that seed

> that sproutit from sapling to a tall tree of girth enough
> to be felled to build its keel? why was it ever oared? (3, 47).

Lochhead's version of *Medea* adheres to its Scottish heritage by revisiting a common motif in Scottish myths and legends, namely the cycle of nature, as it foregrounds the sun's relationship to soil and seed (3). Euripides' recurrent references to the Olympian gods and goddesses in the original play, are replaced by Lochhead's Scottish emphasis on Mother Earth and Sun:

> CHORUS
> Gods stop her if Gods you are!
> Mother Earth open up and swallow her now
> before she forever defiles you
> with the spilt blood of her own children
> the eye of the Sun that is too bright to look upon
> look down stop her in her tracks (43).

The use of Scottish diction contributes to Lochhead's announcement of a Scottish perspective. For instance the three characters, the NURSE, the Manservant and Kreon, have distinctly Scottish accents while the rest of the characters speak standard English. The NURSE and the Manservant (Lochhead's version of the Tutor in Euripides' *Medea*), are the two characters who always speak with a Scottish accent:

> NURSE
> what did you hear?
>
> MANSERVANT
> I'm saying naething
>
> NURSE
> tell me what you heard
>
> MANSERVANT
> to say naething is already to have said too much. (5)

As the audience is introduced to the other characters and incidents after learning these two characters's perspectives on them, the two characters's perspectives become very central to the play. In this respect the Scottish context of the play is further asserted. The NURSE's address to the Manservant foregrounds their difference from the other characters.

> speak to me we're slaves
> baith in the same sair place in this catastrophe. (5)

They are both inhabitants of the land, which is what they have in common with Kreon, as the stage directions suggest. (11) However unlike Kreon, the NURSE and the Manservant are slaves. In other words, the NURSE and the Manservant are addressed as the colonized Other, displaying the play's explicit interest in the issue of self and Other. On the other hand, King Kreon, to whom the stage directions attribute both modesty and power (11), is the only authority figure. That "his voice is strongly Scots" (11) may be related to the Scottish claim of their own indigenism. In his first address to Medea, Kreon is quite assertive of his power in the land:

> ... I banish you
> take your bairns and away you go
> right now far from our borders
> I make the laws and execute them
> only when you're gone will I sleep easy. (11)

The use of the word "border" which has become a postcolonial term after Gloria Anzaldua's *Borderlands: La Frontera* (please view Chapter 2 for details) implies that Kreon stands for the "Other side of the border" where "los atravesados live" (Anzaldua 25), signifying the fantasy of a just Scottish rule in the land. The following lines by Kreon foreground his tyranny,

> KREON:
> I'm no a barbarian I'm no a tyrant either
> but by showing saftness
> I've sometimes been the one to suffer for it in the past. (14)

as they provide a depiction of Kreon as a soft figure of authority. In this respect Kreon's depiction is quite reminiscient of that of Father Winter who in Scottish mythology is associated with both kindness and authority (MacKenzie 35). In one of the myths, Father Winter challenges Beira as she tries to enslave Princess Bride in order to prevent her marriage with Angus the Summer King (MacKenzie 33-35). Lochhead's Kreon plays a similar role in his above quoted warnings to prevent Medea's revenge on Jason and Glauke (11), in a milder tone than Euripides' Creon:

> Medea, I order you to leave my territories
> An exile, and take along with you your two children,
> And not to waste time doing it. It is my decree,
> And I will see it done. I will not return home
> Until you are cast from the boundaries of my land. (19)

The above lines set forth that Euripides' Creon is much more assertive than Lochhead's Kreon, whose address to Medea is quoted on the previous page of this work. Hence it may be suggested that Lochhead's refiguration of Euripides' Creon involves some affinities to Scottish myths and legends in which a mild figure of authority is quite recurrent..

As for Medea, Lochhead's representation of Medea is much more complicated than the original one. Euripides' Medea is motivated to avenge her husband's adultery as a woman while Lochhead's Medea has another significant motivation, namely her ethnic oppression. Although Lochhead's Medea has no single line in Scots, she is explicitly Other'ed in stage directions like "a foreigner speaking good English" (6). Moreover, Medea is quite conscious of her situation as an outsider and she frequently refers to that. For instance, in her address to the Chorus, below, Medea relates her lack of people's love, to her different ethnic background:

> no one loves a foreigner
> everyone despises anyone the least bit different
> ...
> "why can't she be a bit more like us?"
> say you Greeks who bitch about other Greeks
> for not being Greeks from Corinth! (9)

Similarly, Lochhead's Medea assumes that Jason betrayed her for not being local,

> what it is is this a senior statesman
> with a foreign wife a savage I'm an embarrassment
> to you, (20)

in adherence to the Euripidian original:

> ...No, you thought it was not respectable
> As you got on in years to have a foreign wife. (Euripides 31)

Yet Lochhead's play offers a critical stance in addressing the conventional implications of Medea's "foreign" identity as a source of "embarrassment" rather than disrespect. The "foreign" and "savage" wife of Jason, Lochhead's Medea, signifies the colonial Other.

The story of *Medea* is quite similar to that of *Beira, Queen of Winter,* which provides Lochhead with easier access to the Scottish background. Both myths depict the wild and rebellious nature of two women whose search for revenge and power outweighs their love of their children. Like Medea, who victimizes her children, using them as an instrument for gaining revenge on Jason,...

> JASON
> Oh, children I loved!
>
> MEDEA
> I loved them. You did not.
>
> JASON
> You loved them, and killed them.
>
> MEDEA
> To make you feel pain (Euripides 63-64)

...Beira engages in battle with her own son, Angus the King of Summer, because she wants to control all the seasons. In the following lines, Beira makes a call to her servants to move the clouds: "Ride southward with me, all of you, and scatter our enemies before us" (MacKenzie 45). The above quote indicates that in a search for power, Beira considers her own son as one of her "enemies." Thus, it is possible to trace Lochhead's rewriting of *Medea,* also to a revisitation of the Scottish version of the myth of a cruel mother. In all these respects, Lochhead's rewriting of Euripides' *Medea* reflects a Scottish perspective not only with the use of Scottish diction but also with its incorporation of the Scottish oral tradition. The play also announces its postcolonial stance by foregrounding the issue of self and Other through its reduction of standard English to a minor language; in Lochhead's own words in her Foreword to the play, by "give[ing] the dominant mainstream society a Scottish tongue." (2) Lochhead's rewriting of Sophocles' *The Theban Plays* links Oedipus's story to that of Antigone within the structure of the same play. Lochhead's play consists of two parts: "Oedipus"and "Jocasta/Antigone." As Lochhead mentions in her note to the play, her version entitled *Thebans* also retells "bits of *The Phoenician Women*" by Euripides.

Sophocles' *The Theban Plays* deals with the fall of the royal house of Thebes. In *Oedipus the King*, the time when Oedipus becomes the ruler of Thebes by solving the riddle of the sphinx, is represented. While Oedipus tries to learn the reason for the famine in Thebes, together with the reader, he learns that he had killed his father and married his mother. Oedipus was in charge of both acts, unknowingly, as in infancy he was sent away from home in fear that he would kill his father and thus fulfill the Oracle's prophecy. As she learns the truth, Jocasta, his mother, commits suicide and Oedipus blinds himself and leaves Thebes. *Oedipus at Colonus* represents Oedipus's arrival at Colonus, together with his daughters Antigone and Ismene (from his marriage with Jocasta). Oedipus dies and a strife begins between Polyneices and Eteocles, the two sons of Oedipus and Jocasta. *Antigone* is another tragedy in which Antigone is depicted in a Dilemma: either she lets her brother Polyneices's body lie unburied, or she buries him against the will of King Creon (as he considers Polyneices a traitor) and is sentenced to death. As she buries the corpse, Antigone commits suicide. Creon's decision to release Antigone is announced too late and the tragedy is followed by two other suicides: Haemon, Antigone's fiancee and Creon's son, and Haemon's mother.

The Phoenician Women deals with the story of several women from Phoenicia, who are trapped by the war in Thebes while on their way to Delphi. The Phoenician women are not characterized individually, but represented stereotypically, as the Greek chorus, so that the play can display how common people are victimized by war. The play initially introduces Jocasta, who in Euripides' version has not commited suicide. It may be useful to give a summary of the plot of *The Phoenician Women* in order to foreground its difference from Sophocles' version. The play starts with Jocasta's brief account of Oedipus's story and states that after Oedipus blinded himself, Eteocles and Polyneices hid him so that people would forget about the events. Since Oedipus cursed the two sons saying that one of them would kill the other for the throne, Eteocles and Polyneices try to agree on ruling the country for a year each. However Eteocles does not obey the plan and wants his brother to be exiled. As Polyneices, who is soon saved from exile, reclaims Thebes, a war starts between the two brothers. The play also represents the attempts of Jocasta and Antigone to stop the war. As the war ends with the death of both sons, Jocasta commits suicide. Creon forbids the burial of Polyneices in Thebes, claiming that he was a traitor. Antigone rebels against the order and breaks off her engagement with Haemon who is Creon's son. The play ends as Antigone and Oedipus depart for exile together.

Lochhead's *Thebans* generally adheres to the story of Sophocles' *The Theban Plays* in Part 1 while it partially follows that of Euripides' *The Phoenician Women* in Part 2. Part 1 opens with Oedipus's address to the people of Thebes, as in Sophocles' version, and is followed by the reply of the Chorus. In adherence to Sophocles' play, in Part 1 both Oedipus and Jocasta learn the truth and Oedipus blinds himself. However in Part 2 that is called 'Jocasta/Antigone', Jocasta is still alive. As in Euripides' version, Jocasta first summarizes Oedipus's story and later, with the help of her daughters, Ismene and Antigone, urges her two sons , Polyneices and Eteocles, to make peace. Part 2 which continues with the two brothers's fight and Antigone's challenge to Creon about the burial of her brother's body, ends with Antigone's and Haemon's suicides. In other words, Part 2 begins with the story of Euripides' play in relation to Jocasta but proceeds with Sophocles' version in relation to Antigone.

Thebans rewrites the myths of Thebes by incorporating both Sophocles' and Euripides' versions. The play broadly deals with the themes of self and Other, human oppression and the destructive use of power. It should be noted that Lochhead's *Thebans* offers a strong feminist perspective in revisiting these two early stories of Thebes, which is further studied in Chapter 6. Unlike in *Medea*, Lochhead does not foreground any Scottish context in *Thebans* which possibly accounts for the reason why the latter has a remarkably less postcolonial bent.

However, *Thebans* introduces a few aspects which are noteworthy from a post-colonial perspective as well.

> It is hard to think of a time in human history when
> these plays wouldn't seem to be prescient and contemporary,
> but in our apocalyptic days as, in a great city at the heart of
> the most powerful empire in the world, towers were razed to
> the ground, as a new plague spread, as the people of Iraq waited
> for the overwhelming might of the enemy to be unleashed upon
> them, as the Palestinias saw that the Israelis would concede nothing
> to stop the fighting, as a ruler found himself locked into a scenario
> where he couldn't lose face, as we all waited for a war to begin which
> we were powerless to stop, it was hard not to feel that the Euripides
> who wrote Jocasta's great plea to her sons to step back from the brink
> was, uncannily writing about and just for us, here, now.

In the above quote, taken from her note to *Thebans*, Lochhead argues that the destructive search for power and its oppression of innocent people, are a matter for all times. Especially the last lines invite the reader to bring into the text a contemporary context of ethnic and colonial oppression. In her interview with Gonzalez Lochhead suggests that it is her intention to adapt the old stories to contemporary contexts so as to show that the stories are "universal": "I am not really a translator, I am an adapter, and I am just making versions of Greek plays that there have been many versions of [...] to show that the plays are not stuck in a context." (102)

In Lochhead's modernized version of the myths of Thebes, the play opens with a remark on the oppression of innocent people because of the deeds of their rulers. The The Chorus's addresss to Oedipus supports this idea.

> CHORUS
> Oedipus King Oedipus
> here we are young old
> mothers fathers priests
> lovers ordinary folk
> all of us suffering barely containing our panic
> waves of it rising in our breasts how shall we
> survive? (3)

As the above lines are meant to indicate the helplessness and grief of common people, in Lochhead's play the Chorus replies to Oedipus, replacing the Priest in Sophocles' version. In this respect Lochhead's play rewrites the following address to Oedipus, subverting its signs of class stratification.

> PRIEST: My lord and king: we gathered here, as you see,
> Young and old, from the tenderest chicks to the age-bent seniors;
> Priests—I of Zeus—and the pick of our young manhood.
> More sit in the marketplace, carrying boughs like these,
> And around the twin altars of Pallas and the sacred ambers
> Of divination, beside the river of Ismenus.
> (Sophocles, [translated by xx] 26),

For instance, in Lochhead's play the Chorus initially addresses Oedipus simply as "Oedipus" while in Sophocles' play he is called "My lord and king," implying hierarchy. Similarly, Lochhead alternates the Priest's consideration of Oedipus as "the first of men" (Sophocles 26) by making her Chorus ironically remind Oedipus of the significance of the citizens: "[...W]ithout Thebans what is Thebes?" (4). In Lochhead's play, the Chorus also calls Oedipus "our King-elect" (4), which further indicates that Lochhead has reshaped the political life of Thebes, bringing them democracy instead of tyranny.

Lochhead's play parodies Sophocles' and Euripides' plays also by treating the epic qualities of the plays in mock seriousness. This aspect of the play reinforces its overall postmodern discourse of self and Other, challenging the notion of a centralized power. For instance, Lochhead's play involves an ironic stance with respect to Sophocles' depiction of an omnipotent Oedipus at the beginning of his play. In the following conversation, Oedipus asks for another riddle so that he can still be the "saviour" of Thebes (4). However Tiresias's answer is ironic, as Oedipus notes.

> OEDIPUS: Another riddle.
> TIRESIAS: solve this one.
> OEDIPUS: mock all you want that's the skill
> that made me King
> TIRESIAS: the criminal is here now with me
> the stranger to the city who is his native son
> the rich man who'll be a beggar with a blind
> man's stick
> his children's brother and father
> his mother's son and lover
> his father's son heir and slayer
> See if you can solve that one and it'll drive you
> blind (Lochhead 12)

The above reduction of the long descriptive language of the conversation below is another sign of such an attitude:

> OEDIPUS: Man, you must still wrap up your words in riddles?
> TIRESIAS: Were you not famed for skill in solving riddles?
> OEDIPUS: You taunt me with the gift that is my greatness?
> TIRESIAS: Your great misfortune, and your ruin. (Sophocles 38)

Similarly, in Part 2 Jocasta's initial address to the Olympian gods is parodied, announcing a subversion of oppressive power relations among men and the Olympians, in Greek myths.

> JOCASTA: O sun-god, who cleavest thy way along the starry sky,
> mounted on golden-studded car, rolling on thy path of
> flame behind fleet coursers, how curst the beam thou didst
> shed on Thebes, the day that Cadmus left Phoenicia's
> realm beside the sea and reached this land! (Euripides 3)

The above quote refers to the sun-god in both admiration and fear of a superior power, while the quote below, ironically challenges his power.

> JOCASTA: old sun in the sky
> you see it all eh?
> you shine on regardless
> that big bright eye of yours un-

> blinking are you mocking us
> or what? have you no mercy?
> don't blush just fire up
> and see the old ball rolling once again
> why not?
> another day another dawn
> so snuff every small star
> long long ago were you watching?
> yes you must have hung there
> bold as brass in the bright blue sky
> when Cadmus fetched up here from far
> Phoenicia
> ended up in this cursed spot
> one fine day that had the nurve to not
> look doomed at all (32)

The former quote depicts the sun-god as a decision-maker cursing Thebes deliberately, in contrast to the latter which questions the omniscience of the sun-god in relation to the tragic incidents taking place in Thebes. Furthermore the tone and the language used in the above quotes, signify a creed in, respectively, the presence and absence of power structures. For instance the former quote involves a strong obedience to the sun-god reflected by its address in a highly elevated language while the latter displays a rebellion against the sun-god, involving an ironic as well as colloquial tone. Recalling the Apollo-Marsyas myth which demonstrates the tragic outcomes of a mortal's challenge to an immortal (see Chapter 3) and viewing the above quote from *Thebans*, one can suggest that Lochhead's play subverts the signs of hierarchical oppression embedded in Western myths.

In all these respects Lochhead's *Thebans* can be considered as a noteworthy rewriting of the Theban myths of oppression. Subverting their conventional representations of hierarchical power structures, Lochhead revisits the two classical stories of Thebes and uses the medium of fiction to liberate their oppressed characters. Lochhead's modernized version of the two Theban myths also owns a post-colonial perspective in relating these classical stories to the contemporary experience of postcolonial oppression.

Liz Lochhead's rewritings of *Medea* and *Thebans* structurally adhere to their content. For instance, Lochhead's use of Scottish diction in her version of *Medea*, a play that she writes in English, goes parallel to her Scottish postcolonial stand. As mentioned before, Lochhead centralizes the minor characters of the Euripidean *Medea* in her version and gives them Scottish diction. The use of Scots signifies a Scottish resistance to the standard English spoken by the mainstream of Scottish society. In this respect Lochhead's *Medea* is reflective of "the big split in Scotland" which in Emily Todd's interview Lochhead describes as "between self and other self" (122). Lochhead's play positively responds to Ian Crichton Smith's call for a Scottish self-confrontation in the following poem:

> Let our three voiced country
> Sing in a new world
> joining to the other rivers without dogma,
> But with friendliness to all around her.
>
> Let her river shine on a day
> That is fresh and glittering and contemporary;
> Let it be true to itself and to its origins
> inventive, original, philosophical,
> its institutions mirror its beauty:
> Then without shame we can esteem ourselves.

By both revisiting early Greek texts and employing some Scottish and Celtic mythical background, Lochhead's texts represent their own Scottish in-between identities; in-between their own European textualities and their Otherness to the mainstream Western canon. Thus Lochhead displays an attitude "true to itself and to its origins" in accordance with Crichton Smith's suggestion. Lochhead's adaptations follow the plot lines of the Greek classics which have become the codes of the Western canon. By offering new backgrounds—namely Scottish and contemporary ones—for the same story, Lochhead also challenges the ancient Euripidean and Sophoclean plays. As she juxtaposes two different Greek stories of Thebes in an ironic tone, Lochhead celebrates her structurally hybrid text coming out of the two texts, Sophocles' *The Theban Plays* and Euripides' *The Phonecian Women*, the stories of which are Others of each other.

5.2. A Postcolonial Perspective to Cherrie L. Moraga's *The Hungry Woman: A Mexican Medea* and *Heart of the Earth: A Popul Vuh Story*

Cherrie L. Moraga's The Hungry Woman:

A Mexican Medea is a very striking play, challenging both colonial and heterosexual codes of oppression. Besides its lesbian feminist stance, Moraga's *Medea* reflects a very strong postcolonial discourse and offers an authentic incorporation of Indian myths into an old Greek story.

The playwright's note to the play announces to its reader/audience an inevitable postcolonial context indicating that "[a]n ethnic civil war has 'balkanized' about half of the United States into several smaller nations of people," namely Africa-America, the Mechicano Nation of Aztlan, the Union of Indian Nations, the Hawai'i Nation; and the confederacy of First Nations Peoples in the former state of Alaska. (6) Medea is among the revolutionaries who rebel against the ongoing oppressive political and economic system in the States, in Moraga's words, "the Euro-American cultural domination of all societal matters." (6) Thus Medea, whom the playwright's notes introduce as "a leader in the Chicano revolt" is exiled after the revolt. (6)

Moraga's version shares little with Euripides' *Medea* in story and plot. Moraga's play is thoroughly a Mexicanized version of Medea as its title, "The Hungry Woman: A Mexican Medea," implies. The play adheres to the classical Greek story of Medea in terms of Medea's exile and her fall after killing her own son but differs from it in a crucial way. In Moraga's version of the story, it is not Jason who betrays Medea but Medea who betrays Jason with Luna, her lesbian lover. Moraga's play also excludes some significant characters from Euripides' *Medea*, namely Creon and one of Medea's sons, yet it introduces its own original characters such as Luna, Mama Sal, Savannah and its own versions of Medea, Nurse, Jason and Medea's son (called Chac-Mool in Moraga's play). The stage directions introduce the four Cihuatateo (El Coro) as a

> [c]horus of four warrior women who, according [to] the Aztec myth, have died in childbirth. Here they are identified with four directions and four primary Pre-Columbian colors. EAST(Red), NORTH (Black), WEST (White), and SOUTH (Blue). The figures wear the faces of the dead in the form of skulls. Their hands are shaped into claws. Their breasts appear bare and their

> skirts are tied with the cord of snake. They are barefoot, their
> ankles wrapped in shell rattles. The chorus performs in the
> traditional style of Aztec danzantes (8)

and it replaces the classical Greek chorus. The Cihuatateo's address to the reader/audience is even prior to that of the Nurse, which displays a subversion of the original play from the very beginning:

> CIHUATATEO EAST:
> This is how all stories begin and end
> the innocence of an eagle feather
> stuffed inside a mother's apron.
>
> The birdboy growing there
> taking shape.
> The warrior son waiting in the wings
> taking flight.
>
> So, too begins and ends this story.
> The birth of a male child
> From the dark sea of Medea
> at the dawning of an age.
>
> [CIHUATATEO NORTH crosses to CIHUATATEO EAST
> and hands her a red NURSE's cap. As she puts it on, NORTH
> covers her own face in a black ski mask.]
>
> NURSE: This is how all days begin and end. (9)

Introducing Cihuatateo before the Nurse, Moraga foregrounds an Indian atmosphere, accompanied by "Pre-Columbian Meso-American music." (9) These four Aztec figures who represent the ancient roots, together play a transitional role in the play's shift to the past. Unlike *Medea*, Moraga's play follows a non-linear plot line, its structure adhering to its own postcolonial content. In an interview, Moraga accounts for the "nonprogressive" plot line in *The Hungry Woman* by calling it a "conscious" deviation from "Eurocentricism or Euro-Americanism" and an attempt to "think outside their structures" (2006:134). In this respect, the non-linearity of Moraga's play challenges the Aristotelian notion of the unity of time and in turn the structures of the entire Western canon. The story of Moraga's Medea is presented through shifts between past and present, representing both colonial history and its influence on contemporary times. Because according to Moraga "...myth is the same with story and history is a part of the story" (2006:134).

The incidents take place a few years after the exile during which Medea along with her son Chac-mool and her lover Luna had to live in the remains of Phoenix, Arizona, away from their country, Aztlan. Through retrospective techniques, the reader/audience learns that Medea was exiled for betraying her husband Jason by having a lesbian relationship with Luna. Medea has also killed Jason's son Chac-mool to prevent his betrayal of his maternal ties with Aztlan by becoming a man and adapting the "macho" attitude of Azlan . At present, Medea is in a "prison psychiatric ward," (6) often visited by her memories of Luna, Chac-mool and Jason. The hospital is in "what remains of Phoenix, Arizona, located in a kind of metaphysical border region between Gringolandia (U.S.A.) and Aztlan (Mechicano country)." (6) Moraga's remark on the notion of "border" contributes to the centralization of a postcolonial Chicano context, reminiscent of the following definition by Gloria Anzaldua:

> 1, 950 mile-long open wound
> Diving a pueblo, a culture,
> running down the length of my body,
> staking fence rods in my flesh,
> splits me splits me
> me raja me raja
>
> This is my home
> this thin edge of
> barbwire. (25)

In the above quote, Anzaldua considers the Chicano life on the "borderline" as a fragmented experience—because the border disintegrates or "splits" one's conception of an overall identity, problematizing the location of one's "culture" and thus metaphorically challenging the unity of one's "body." The last lines reflect a stronger postcolonial discourse in calling the defamiliarizing "edge of barbwire," the Chicano "home." That is where Moraga also locates the *pueblo* in "The Hungry Woman: A Mexican Medea." The following conversation among three Chicana(o) characters is about their new home where they settled after the Chicano revolt:

> SAVANNAH: And we made a kind of gypsy ghetto for ourselves in what was once a thriving desert.
> MAMA SAL: They call it "Phoenix,",pero entrenos, we name it "Tamoanchan," which means-
> CHAC-MOOL: "We seek our home"
> MAMA SAL: And the seeking itself becomes our home. (24)

The above lines indicate that while living in the States, the Chicano home is located always on the border, which metaphorically refers to their considerations of their home as ever home-seeking. The conversation below implies that the Chicano(a)s belong to neither side of the border:

> BORDER GUARD: I'm trying to ascertain your readiness to make the return.
>
> CHAC-MOOL: I don't want to be here no more.
> BORDER GUARD: Where?
> CHAC-MOOL: Tamoachan.
> BORDER GUARD: Phoenix?
> CHAC-MOOL: Yes.
> BORDER GUARD: Where do you want to be?
> CHAC-MOOL: Aztlan. (76-77)

The lines above suggest that Chac-Mool is neither truly an American as he still calls Phoenix "Tamoachan," nor a Mexican as he has to prove his "readiness to make the return" to Aztlan possible. The following quote asserts that crossing the border is ever forbidden for the Chican(o)as:

> BORDER GUARD: Why did you cross the border?
> LUNA: I was on my way to her.
> BORDER GUARD: To whom?
> LUNA: I got distracted
> ...
> BORDER GUARD: But you hadn't a work permit.
> LUNA: I was denied one.
> BORDER GUARD: You knew it was illegal
> LUNA: Yes.
> BORDER GUARD: Then-
> LUNA: I longed for Aztlan. (61)

The above quote may be taken, metaphorically, as an indicator of the impossibility of a true reconciliation with either side of the identities. In this respect, border crossing stands for confrontation with hybridity itself. This aspect of the play adheres to Homi K. Bhabha's conception of hybridity as an "in-between space", led by the encounter of the colonizer and the colonized, which inevitably challenges any means of having a "fixed"cultural identity, but rather offers a process of "translation and negotiation," a "third space" (40-43). Moraga's rewriting of Euripides' *Medea* foregrounds the Chicano sense of "in-betweenness" with a postcolonial insight. The play accomplishes the representation of the "in-between"

103

space on the "borderline" by tracing the hybrid Chicano(a) roots to both their Aztec origins as Mexicans and their Euro-American ancestry. The bilingual structure of the play also enhances the postcolonial context, centralizing the notion of hybridity. The incorporation of Spanish words and phrases in an English sentence, announces the language of the text as Chicano. Reflecting a culture which is already in-between American and Mexican Cultures, the language is inevitably hybrid or bilingual:

> MAMA SAL: Tu mama y su cadre were one among many small groups organizing revolts in pueblitos throughout the Southwest.
> Then Los Independistas declared Vieques Island free and sovereign-
> SAVANNAH: Which inspired an international response, already spearheaded by the Mayas in Chiapas.
> CHAC-MOOL: The Zapatistas.
> NURSE: O-69.
> MAMA-SAL: The Zapatistas took on the PRI and the PAN y hasta el partido de la TORTILLA and the Mexican president got
> shot and bueno... the rest is history. Pan-indigenismo
> tore America apart and Aztlan was born from the
> pedacitos.
> SAVANNAH: Uniting the disenfranchised diaspora of Indian-mestizos throughout the southwest. (23)

The above conversation exemplifies the smooth shift between English and Spanish which seems to be the natural language of the Chicano(a)s represented in the play. Given the above context of an ethnic revolt "uniting" "Indian-mestizos," such a use of language adheres structurally to the postcolonial content of the conversation.

Moraga's incorporation of Aztec myths and legends into the play contributes to the postcolonial discourse embedded in her rewriting of *Medea*. Chac-mool and Luna's names, for instance, both refer to Aztec mythology. While Chac-mool, according to I. Mayorga, stands for "the messenger between this world and the other" (160), Luna is reminiscient of the Aztec goddess Coyolxauhqui who, according to a pre-columbian myth, was killed by the fetus of her brother, Huitzilopochtli (identified with the sun), in their mother Coatlicue's womb. As Huitzilopochtli cuts off Coyolxauhqui's limbs and tosses her head into the sky, Coyolxauhqui becomes the moon, La Luna (160-162). Act 2 also starts with the "illumination" of the image of Coatlicue, the Aztec Goddess of Creation and Destruction on the stage. The Cihuatateo stand beside the Goddess and the background is "semi-dark" (Moraga 55). As the stage directions further state, Medea emerges from the icon sweeping, in the image of Coalticue (Moraga 55). In the meantime Cihuatateo East starts telling her version of Coatlicue's story while Luna appears on the stage as Coyolxauqui. The Aztec Goddess, Coatlicue becomes a noteworthy central image on the stage even at the very beginning, as noted in the Prelude (9), which modifies Euripides' recurrent references to the Olympians. The description of the Aztec goddess in "a serpent skirt" (9), possibly signifying the female generative power on earth, inevitably requires a reference to Aztec mythology in which "Earth is a coiled Serpent" (Anzaldua 48). The Aztec myth of The Hungry Woman, La Llorona, is also revisited in the play, as another challenge to the dominantly Greek context of *Medea*. The myth of La Llorona deals with the oppressive power relations at the times when the earth had not yet been created. As it involves feminist themes, the myth of La Llorona will be studied further in Chapter 5. However it should be noted that the Aztec myth of La Llorona, the Hungry Woman, is a significant myth, reflecting the oppression of female body in a male-dominated world. In this respect, there is a noteworthy similarity of plot between the Aztec myth of La Llorona and the Greek myth of Philomela which in turn can be traced to a common female experience. The fact that Moraga situates an Aztec myth, not a Greek one, dealing with oppression at the centre of her play, implies a challenge to oppressive power structures. In other words, Moraga's play subverts the hegemonies to which Euripides' *Medea* conforms, in part by privileging the Aztec myths over their European counterparts. In this respect the play treats the Aztec heritage as a means of spiritual liberation against the ethnic oppression the Chicano(a)s have been exposed to.

The Mayan epic, *Popul Vuh*, was originally written in hieroglyphics but its transcription from oral literature to the Roman alphabet dates back to the mid-16th century. The Mayan myth also introduces an old creed system in Mayan culture as it offers an ancient story of creation. *Popul Vuh* has an episodic structure in two parts, the first of which takes place on earth while the second takes place in the underworld. The book was translated into English by Dennis Tedlock, who notes the authentic structure of *Popul Vuh* which does not follow a chronological order but rather owns a spatial concern in its division of the "two different cycles":

> If the events of these two cycles were combined in a
> single chronological sequence, the above-ground episodes
> would probably alternate with those below, with the heroes
> descending into the underworld, emerging on earth again,

> and so forth. These sowing and dawning movements of the
> heroes, along with those of their supporting cast, prefigure
> the present-day movements of the sun, moon, planets and
> stars. (35-36)

With an emphasis on the "movements of the sun, moon, planets and stars", the above quote by Tedlock foregrounds the Mayan background of astronomy and astrology, which symbolically links the present to future. Leon-Portilla remarks that the pre-Columbian cultures were so "advanced," especially "in their knowledge of astronomy, mathematics and chronology," that it is no wonder "they have developed an extraordinary cosmology, constructing a complex mythological system for symbolic explanation." (28) In this respect, the non-linear structure of *Popul Vuh* along with the "sowing and dawning movements" of its characters may be taken as a symbolic reflection of this extraordinary cosmology, signifying a cyclical understanding of time . This view accounts for the Mayan consideration of *Popul Vuh* as a "seeing instrument of past and future," (Tedlock 32) which also implies the interconnection of all times.

Cherrie Moraga's act of rewriting *Popul Vuh* announces an attempt to foreground the uncanonized Mayan creation myth as opposed to its canonized Western counterparts, the versions of the myth of Genesis. *Heart of the Earth* incorporates the first four parts of *Popul Vuh* in which are depicted the attempts of two Mayan deities, the god Ixpiyacoc and the goddess Ixmucane, to create the earth, animals and human beings, respectively. *Heart of the Earth*, Moraga's version of *Popul Vuh,* represents the process in which the ancient Mayan deities, Ixpiyacoc, Ixmucane and Cucumatz, create the world. *Heart of the Earth* also depicts the journey to the underworld of the twin brothers', Hunaphu and Vucub, and their victimization by the Patriarchal Pus and Blood Sausage, the two oppressive gods of Xibalba, the Mayan underworld. Adhering to the episodic structure of *Popul Vuh*, the incidents in *Heart of Earth* repeat themselves with the next generation's twins, Hunahpu and Ixbalanque.

Moraga's version of the play deals with the first four parts of the Mayan epic from postcolonial and feminist perspectives, the latter of which will be discussed in Chapter 6. Adhering to Moraga's ultimate goal as suggested in the playwright's note to the play, *Heart of the Earth* offers a strong postcolonial perspective in its treatment of the indigenous cultures in America:

> I have tried to create a version of the *Popul Vuh* which honors its original language, while acknowledging that Quiche is a living language used not only among the Maya in the highlands of Guatemala, but can also be heard [sic] on the streets of New York City, along with Quechua, Nahuatl, Navajo, Lakota and a myriad of other Indigenous American tongues. As *Heart of the Earth* is being presented in the U.S., the world of language I hope to evoke is one of a diverse and people-of-color America that more closely reflects its changing and beautifully darkening face as we enter the 21st century. (104)

The play's multi-lingual structure which involves "standard English and Spanish, Quiche, other Mayan tongues, Spanglish, Chicano speech from the Southwest, and the urban colloquialisms of U.S. city streets" (Moraga 104), reinforces its postcolonial content. The play provides a vivid representation of the indigenous community speaking these languages which are the Others of standard English. In this respect, the play strongly reflects *Chicanismo* which Gomez-Quinones defines as an evoking of "Mexican cultural consciousness and heritage as well as pride in speaking [the] Spanish language" (104).

Heart of the Earth opens with the Daykeeper, a contemporary figure functioning as the story-teller, who plays a transitional role between contemporary time and the time of ancient Maya. Her initial address to the reader/audience announces the story as "[…] the story of how light was born from darkness y la luz shadowed again by the hands of the gods" (Moraga 107). However the Daykeeper also plays the role of the postcolonial critic as she raises a postcolonial consciousness in her reader/audience: "We shall tell our cuento en voz alta for there is no place to read it" (107). The Daykeeper then reminds the reader/audience of the context of postcolonial oppression: "Five hundred years ago, the bearded ones arrived in floating palacios, in search of sun's golden secretions. They came armed with flechas of melded steel and a black book decrying their devil. *(Pause)*" (107) As the Daykeeper is contemporary to the 1990s, the time when *Heart of the Earth* was written, her reference to the incidents taking place "five hundred years ago" refers to the time when America was discovered by white men. After the pause, the Daykeeper relates their arrival to the reason why "[t]oday our children know fewer and fewer Indian prayers; they put on a Ladino cloth of soldier and seller" (107). Given this context, the pause before the above quote functions as a gap which in turn serves as a postmodern strategy meant to make the reader/audience fill it in.

The postcolonial content of the play is reinforced as the Daykeeper finally suggests that, "...our book and its author keep their faces hidden" (107), and she becomes Ixmucane, wearing the god-headdress Ixpiyacoc carries. Irma Mayorga traces Moraga's strategy of "theatrical disposition" to the "Chicana/o equivalent" of the "daykeeper's task" in early Mayan tradition (163). To Mayorga, Moraga "reanimates" the morale of the stories in the book, providing "a new performance" from a "contemporary" perspective, similar to "the daykeepers" or "diviners" who offer "their oral interpretations of the world's creation by weaving the book's [*Popul Vuh's*] astronomical charts, pictures, plot outlines, and glyphs into story for an audience." (163)

The second play of the *Heart of the* Earth centralizes the Mayan gods of creation as well as their Others, the Lords of the underworld. The play places them on two sides of the binary pole as the indigenous corn-planters with "red" skin and the unearthly oppressors with "pale" (Moraga 115) skin. While the red ones can speak their languages, those from the underworld are authoritatively monolingual speakers of English. Their "(mispronunc-e-)" [iation] of the Spanish word "co-MO-da", which is highlighted by the playwright in parenthetical citations (119), implies their authoritative and oppressive attitudes. In other words, the relationship between the two different communities in the play can be traced to what Edward Saïd called power, domination, and "varying degrees of a complex hegemony," (5). The issue of the one and the Other is foregrounded in the play through a representation of ethnic or racial stratification. In contrast to the oppressive Lords of the underworld who victimize the first generation twins for "fresh blood" (115) as "they want everyone empty and blood-gray like them" (122), the gods of creation "love all their children" (122).

> At the crossroads, all colors converge: el colorado,el negro, el amarillo y el blanco.
> Pero encontraran su destino on that blood-black road of Xibalba. (117)

Moraga's play openly displays a Chicano(a) postcolonial context, as announced by one of the Lords of the underworld/death, Patriarchal Pus, who calls the cell where the twins are enslaved the "South of the Border Theme House" (119). With all their oppressive and aggressive attitudes toward the "red" ones, the Lords of the underworld fit into Gloria Anzaldua's reference to the "Gringos in the U.S. Southwest" as those who view the people from the "borderland" such as "Chicanos,

Indians or Blacks" as "transgressors, aliens." (25) Anzaldua further notes that only the whites and the powerholders have a right to live on the U.S. side of the border and that the life there is full of "tension," "unrest," "ambivalence" and "death" for "the inhabitants of the borderlands." (25-26) The dark depiction of the U.S. side of the border in Anzaldua's lines is quite similar to that of the following lines in which the Lords of Death describe the life in the underworld that they call "home":

> Sudden deaths in subway stations,
> A quick blade to the heart!
> The slow dissolution of body and bone
> by a hunger left in the dark.
>
> Name the disease, we invented it!
> And we daily dream up more!
> Silent plagues are our favourite,
>
> a game of our cellular war.
>
> This is the home of Cizin
> who passes a gruesome gas.
> No one escapes our odornor the call of the water-lilied path. (Moraga 117-118)

In other words, the underworld very possibly represents life on the U.S. side of the border and the Lords of Death stand for its oppressive dominant white ruling. In this respect, it can be suggested that *Heart of the Earth* engages in a strong postcolonial discourse in its treatment of the Mexican-American issue. The play's content also foregrounds the hybrid backgrounds of the Chicano(a). For instance corn, which signifies the Mexican heritage, plays a significant role in the play as it is the first food the Mayan gods created in *Popul Vuh*. The goddess Ixmucane offers her sons some "fresh tortillas" made of corn, which is a sign of the indigenism of this foodstuff. Besides it is whether or not one can plant corn that determines whether the goddess Ixmucane will define one as an insider or an outsider. When Ixquick, the mother of the second-generation twins, claims that she is Ixmucane's daughter-in-law, Ixmucane tests Ixquick by asking her to make the barren corn field full to Ixmucane (126). When Ixquick accomplishes the task, Ixmucane announces Ixquick as her daughter even though she is an outsider:

> IXMUCANE:... (Seeing the mountain of corn) !Hija benedita!
> El dios de maiz te ha tocado. (She embraces her)
> Daughter of corn and light! Basta! De verdad, eres

> mi hija! Ayudame, mija. (She begins stuffing the corn into the net.) Mi viejo will be thrilled to see que abundancia le trae su nuera a la familia. Con tanto corn, we will surely be busy con la tamalada tonight! (127)

The significance of corn in this context signifies their indigenism to the earth. From a postcolonial perspective, the corn-planting test serves as an instrument to centralize the notion of hybridity as a means of reconciliation. Such understanding of hybridity can be traced to Homi K. Bhabha's suggestion of the "negotiation between the colonizer and the colonized" through the cultural transcription of the hybrid (1994:38). It is through the corn that Ixmucane recognizes the hybridity of her daughter-in-law from the Other country, Xibalba. The following conversation between Ixquick and Hunahpu (the first generation one) indicates that Ixquick is a hybrid:

> HUNAHPU: I said, Ixquic, you shouldn't die of hunger.
> IXQUIC: How do you know my name?
> HUNAHPU: By your color. My father told me... he was right. You are a beautiful earth color, Blood Woman.
> HUNAHPU: No, why do you say that?
> IXQUIC: Here in Xibalba... with the blood-less Lords. They want everyone empty and bone-gray like them
> HUNAHPU: Come to my country. There the Blue-Green Kukulcan reigns. And Ixmucane and Ixpiyacoc, my parents, they love all their children. (122)

That Ixquic has "a beautiful earth color" although she is the daughter of the "pale" Patriarchal Pus, implies a dark maternal heritage. The notion of hybridity is further foregrounded in the play as it is not the first-generation twins (the twin sons of the mayan deities) but the hybrid second-generation ones (the twins of Ixquic and Hunahpu) who accomplish the mission to challenge the oppressive authority in the underworld. As the second-generation twins finally become the sun and the moon, their mother, becomes the sky, offering a path to the earth. In all aspects, Ixquic symbolizes the hybrid Chicano(a) body which is earth-colored (122) and bilingual ("IXQUIC: ...your herencia lives inside me y cuando doy a luz / you will recognize in my children's faces the features of the / sons you mourn" [126]), ever located on the border, "in a constant state of transition" (Anzaldua 25)—both the "daughter of corn" (127) and the daughter of the "blood-less" Devil (122, 121). The foregrounding of the new, mixed race reinforces the idea of a possible "decolonization" which in Wretched of *the Earth* Frantz Fanon argues to be imaginable only in "the creation of new men" (28). *Heart of the Earth* realizes Fanon's fantasy by rewriting the myth of the creation of man and using fiction to decolonize the underworld, freeing it from the oppressors. Furthermore Moraga's play celebrates the mythical decolonization of Aztlan by rewriting the birth of the "people of the sun." In this respect, she asserts the following claim of the Chicano manifesto El Plan Espirituel de Aztlan, which "posits an Aztec/ indigenous origin in [the] Southwestern United States" (Ramirez 49). The following quote which is taken from El Plan Espirituel de Aztlan reflects the revolutionary stand of the Chicanos toward regaining their mythical home, Aztlan:

> In the spirit of a new people that is conscious not only of its proud historical heritage but also of the brutal "gringo" invasion of our territories, we, the Chicano inhabitants and the civilizers of the northern land of Aztlan from whence our forefathers, reclaiming the land of their birth and consecrating the determination of our people of the sun, declare that the call of our blood is our power, our responsibility, and our inevitable destiny. [...] Aztlan belongs to those who plant the seeds, water the fields, and gather the crops and not to the foreign Europeans. (Denver, Colorado, March 1969)

Moraga's multilingual writing foregrounds a Chicano text while her use of a nonlinear plot structure challenges the standard patterns of mainstream literature. In adherence to her hybrid origin as a Chicana, Moraga offers *Hungry Woman: A Mexican Medea* as a bilingual play and *Heart of the Earth: A Popul Vuh Story* as a multilingual one. While *Hungry Woman* incorporates Spanish words and phrases in essentially English sentences, *Heart of the Earth* includes several Mayan tongues, mainly Quiche, and "Spanglish, Chicano speech from the Southwest, and the urban colloquialisms of U.S. city streets besides 'standard English' and Spanish" (104). In other words, the language of Moraga's text may be considered authentically Chicano.

5.3. A Comparative Perspective on Lochhead and Moraga's Representations of Hierarchical and Colonial Oppression

Both Liz Lochhead and Cherrie Moraga own distinctly authentic styles in their revisitations of myths of colonial and hierarchal oppression. The two playwrights not only re-present the old stories of oppression to liberal minds but also represent their challenges to that oppression in their use of alternative dramatic techniques. Their incorporations of Celtic, Scottish and Aztec, Mayan myths into their rewritings of Greek myths also contributes to their authenticity, providing a dialogue between the less known myths and the mainstream Western canon.

On the level of dramatic technique Lochhead challenges the rules of the mainstream Western tradition through her alternative characters and her hybrid text which juxtaposes two different texts. As discussed in 5.2, Lochhead's plays foreground no protagonist with whom the audience is supposed to empathize in the Aristotelian sense. For instance in Lochhead's *Medea* such defamiliarization is attained through the Nurse's self-distancing stance with respect to Medea which breaks the traditional role of the Greek chorus in generating empathy between the protagonist and the audience. Similarly, rewriting *Antigone* as 'Jocasta/Antigone' in *Thebans*, Lochhead announces her allocation of the role of the protagonist to two female characters which in turn introduces two different *hamartia*s. According to the Brazilian critic Augusto Boal, lack of empathy between the protagonist and the audience threatens the final accomplishment of the social purification that Aristotle attributes to tragedy, and thus resists the codes of oppression embedded in tragedies. In other words, the alternative structures used in the two adaptations by Liz Lochhead prevent the possibility of any Aristotelian *catharsis* or *ethos*, the two significant features of classical tragedy which Augusto Boal considers the very essence of a system of oppression (39). In this respect, Liz Lochhead's plays challenge both the conventional representation of oppression and oppressive systems of representation by representing and re-presenting the notion of oppression embedded in classical representations. As the following quote from Jan Mcdonald and Jeniffer Harvey sets forth:

> Lochhead's plays go beyond problematising already
> existent representations as they further encourage their
> audiences to rethink the entire notion of representation

> ...through a persistent metatextuality – a representational
> emphasis on representation itself. (135)

What further contributes to the authenticity of Lochhead's strategy of representation is her challenging attitude in representing the oppression embedded in the classical notion of representation itself. Moraga's plays also adhere to their postcolonial contexts structurally, with their experimental plot lines, which she terms "non-linear and nonprogressive" (2006:134). As Moraga subverts the standard forms of the Western canon which date back to the Aristotelian tradition; she challenges white Eurocentric hegemonies. Moraga's retrospective representation of incidents in *Hungry Woman* or the cyclical one in *Popul Vuh* provide alternative structures, reinforcing her Chicano(a) postcolonial discourse. Similarly, Moraga's plays display problematic representations of space which are related to Anzaldua's notion of *border* in Chapter 6. Moraga's alternative form may be further traced to a challenge to the Aristotelian unity of time and place. In the interview, Moraga notes that she "consciously" started to stage multiple times and spaces as she tried to think outside Western structures (2006:134). As noted in Chapters 3 and 6, the Brazilian critic Augusto Boal argues that the Aristotelian tradition of theatre involves a strong political oppression. According to Boal, the Aristotelian understanding of theatre is a political instrument for preventing the tendencies toward undesirable and illegitimate behaviour (3). Boal's view reinforces the function of Moraga's strategy in revisiting the myths which reflect such systems of oppression and replacing them with their Others. As the critic Yvonne Yarbro-Bejarano suggests, Moraga's plays are reflective of the Chicano theatre's challenge to "the hierarchies hidden in 'universal' Western theatre, particularly those of race and class" (24). Yet Moraga's theatre may be considered an authentic representation of this challenge to oppressive structures; providing an alternative style as well as an innovative version of an old story as she rewrites myths of oppression both in content and in form. Both plays by Moraga represent the codes of ethnic or racial oppression involved in canonized drama on the one hand while on the other, through their postcolonial contexts, they challenge such oppression which leads to the nonrepresentation or noncanonization of Other literatures.

As they revisit myths of oppression, Lochhead and Moraga not only subvert the central themes of old stories but also alternate the conventional forms they have. In other words, both Lochhead and Moraga challenge the hegemonic structures that lead to oppression. However, while Moraga manifests a strong postcolonial discourse by prolaiming her indigenism and reclaiming Aztlan, Lochhead's stance might better be called a Scottish patriotism which reflects an interest in her Scottish roots, rather than a discourse on tracing them. In *Medea*, Lochhead gets closer to a postcolonial stance with her alternation of standard English with Scottish English. Yet in both *Medea* and *Thebans*, Lochhead explicitly reflects a resistance to hierarchal oppression, directing a social criticism toward oppression. As for Moraga, her Chicanismo is interconnected with her colored feminism, which is to be discussed in Chapter 6, and emissions her with political activism.

As for the standardization of white Eurocentric canon, Moraga, as a colored writer, displays her resistance more directly than Lochhead. While Lochhead adheres to the story of Medea but offers a Scottish version, Moraga dethrones Medea in a distinctly Chicana story of the Hungry Woman. In other words, Lochhead's is a Scottish version of Euripides' *Medea*, while Moraga's is a Mexican Medea, as she asserts in the title of her play. Similarly, in *Heart of the Earth*, Moraga takes a similar attitude in recentralizing her ancestors' non-canonized story of creation as opposed to that of the deeply canonized *Genesis*. Yet Lochhead's *Thebans* revisits two Greek myths by both following and juxtaposing their stories and plots. In this respect, both repeating and resisting the Eurocentric structures, Lochhead's plays reflect both her white European ancestry and her noncanonized Scottishness.

6. Revisiting Myths of Gender Oppression

6.1. Lochhead's Mainstream Feminism in *Medea* and *Thebans*

Similar to her original plays which are introduced in Chapter 4, Liz Lochhead's rewritings of Euripides' *Medea* and Sophocles' *The Theban Plays* display her feminist stance against a Scottish background. As suggested in Chapter 5.1, the two adaptations by Lochhead foreground less Scottish patriotism and more social feminist discourse on gender oppression.

Lochhead's *Medea* initially centralizes gender by gendering the stereotypically represented Nurse and Tutor in Euripides' play. In the Dramatis Personae, Euripides introduces the Nurse as "[Medea's nurse]" (Euripides 9) and the Tutor as "[the slave who is the tutor to Medea's two small children] (Euripides 10). However in the first set of stage directions, Lochhead announces the gender of the Nurse as female—"[a] woman is talking to herself and us. This is the NURSE" (3), and that of the Tutor as male by naming him "MANSERVANT" and describing him as "handsome, young and strong" (4). In this respect Lochhead challenges the stereotypical representation of the Tutors as young, beautiful and fragile women (see Chapters 1 and 3 for a detailed background on the stereotypical representation of women in literature) while she also allocates the role of domestic servitude to both genders.

Another challenge to Euripides' play can be observed in Lochhead's stereotypical representation of the major male character, Jason, as macho. Euripides' play introduces Jason in a dilemma between his safety and his marriage. Euripides gives Jason a motivation to leave Medea and marry Creon's daughter, which is to protect himself, Medea and his children as well as to bring his children up "worthily" (Euripides 29). With these words Jason foregrounds his reasons for another marriage:

> What luckier chance could I have come across than this,
> An exile to marry the daughter of the king?
> It was not, —the point that upset you— that I
> Grew tired of your bed and felt the need of a new bride;
> Nor with any wish to outdo your number of children.
> We have enough already. I am quite content. (29)

In Lochhead's version the word "exile" is not used in Jason's account of his decision and is replaced by the word "politics" (19), which in turn signifies Jason's search for power instead of his freedom. In other words, Lochhead represents Jason as a stereotypical man by making him victimize his marriage for his own egocentric concerns. In this respect, Lochhead's play displays Medea's former idealization of such a pragmatic man as a typical example of women's exaggeration of the value of men. Thus the play reinforces the following lines by Virginia Woolf: "Women have served all these centuries as looking-glasses possessing the magic and delicious power of reflecting the figure of man at twice its natural size" (35-36).

Lochhead's version also alters the traditional Greek chorus which represents common sense, with a "*CHORUS OF WOMEN of all times, all ages, classes and professions.*" (7) In Euripides' version the "Chorus of Corinthian women" (14) thoroughly conforms to the rules and values of Greek society although it looks forward to a change. The following demonstrates that the Chorus of Corinthian women is conditioned to act the way it is supposed to act so as to keep a good reputation:

> CHORUS
> Flow backward to your sources, sacred rivers,
> And let the world's great order be reversed.
> It is the thoughts of *men* that are deceitful,
> *Their* pledges that are loose.
> Story shall now turn my condition to a fair one,
> Women are paid their due.
> No more shall evil-sounding fame be theirs. (25)

Although these lines partially echo the femininist ideals, the Chorus fails to show any resistance. Yet Lochhead's Chorus on the other hand reflects a feminist activist gaze in its treatment of Medea's suffering:

> That cry we heard it
> knew it in our bones it curdled our blood too (7)

and

> we are sorry for your sorrow sister
> is that how they cry in Kolchis Medea? (7)

Addressing Medea as "sister" and sharing her sorrow, Lochhead's Chorus both shows empathy towards Medea and tries to raise a feminist consciousness in her:

> we were not born yesterday
> we are all survivors of the sex war
> married women widows divorce
> mistresses wives no virgins here
> marriage over? shame that's the end of it
> so get on with it. (7,8)

In this respect Lochhead's Chorus reflects a true female "solidarity," " bonding" or "sisterhood" which through "the spirit of power in unity" makes it possible "to end sexist oppression" (hooks 44). However, by asking about the way people cry in Kolchis, the Chorus takes the perspective of an outsider; alien to the culture in Kolchis. Although the Chorus consists of women, they are unlike Medea who ,like other women in Kolchis, cries "*from inside*" (7). Unlike the traditional Greek chorus, Lochhead's Chorus does not represent common sense or internalized codes of patriarchy but instead represents the individual and independent voices of all women. The two following citations display, respectively, Euripides' Chorus in conformity with the oppressive codes of patriarchy(except for the chorus leader), and Lochhead's Chorus in a direct challenge to them:

> JASON: But you women have got into such a state of mind
> That, if your life at night is good, you think you have
> Everything; but, if in that quarter things go wrong,
> You will consider your best and truest interests
> Most hateful. It would have been better far for men
> To have got their children in some other way, and women
> Not to have existed. Then life would have been good. .
>
> CHORUS [LEADER]:
> Jason, though you have made this speech of yours look well,
> Still I think, even though others do not agree,
> You have betrayed your wife and are acting badly.
> (Euripides 30)

and

> JASON: ...
> cunts for brains! that's women they're all the same
> happy in the sack and all the world's a bed of clover
> if that goes sour they go spare
> and hate you sex!
> I hope there was another way to get us sons
> without women the world would be a lovely place

117

> CHORUS:
> well said Jason your arguments are clever
> we understand you do your wife a favour
> by dumping her? we beg to differ. (Lochhead 20)

In both versions, Jason displays an oppressive attitude toward women by reducing them to sex and birthing. Euripides' Chorus takes a serious tone in its consideration of Jason's argument as logical, unlike the ironic stance taken by that of Lochhead. The Euripidean Chorus conforms to the patriarchal perspective as it wishes marriage to continue under all circumstances. The following lines which the Chorus utters after Medea's angry response to Jason imply that the Chorus still expects Medea to reconcile herself with Jason: "When members of a family fight like this, rage pushes them beyond all compromise" (Euripides 27-28). That the Chorus calls Medea and Jason "members of a family" also implies a hope for some reconciliation. However, Lochhead's Chorus does not question the ending of Jason and Medea's marriage, under the given conditions.

The recurrent references to Medea's cry "*from inside*" (7) are significant also because they show Medea's repression and resentment. Medea's repetitive cry "*from inside*" (7), might be taken as a sign of women's typical repression of their feelings due to *ressentiment*. Max Scheler writes:

> Ressentiment is a self-poisoning of the mind which has quite
> definite causes and consequences. It is a lasting mental attitude,
> caused by the systematic repression of certain emotions and
> affects which, as such, are normal components of human
> nature. Their repression leads to the constant tendency to
> indulge in certain kinds of value delusions and corresponding
> value judgments. The emotions and affects primarily concerned
> are revenge, hatred, malice, envy, the impulse to detract, and
> spite. (29)

As mentioned in Chapter 1, for Max Scheler's notion of *ressentiment* is closely linked to oppression, the internalization of which leads to a "systematic repression of certain emotions and affects." Because such female gender codes and stereotypes require women to repress the "normal components of human nature," the outcome is a "constant tendency " toward "value delusions." Scheler's theory accounts for Lochhead's Medea's indulging in "value delusions" when she murders her own children and Jason's wife. In other words, Scheler's reader may expect cruel "revenge" from Lochhead's Medea whose cry "*from inside*" is a silent expression of such ongoing repression. The above quote by Scheler may be specifically related to "gender oppression" or "sexist oppression" which the black feminist theorist bell hooks suggests is socially structured "by the individuals who dominate, exploit, or oppress; and by the victims themselves who are socialized to behave in ways that make them act in complicity with the status quo," namely with the "[m]ale supremacist ideology" (43). hooks exemplifies her points with references to the male-centered views such as "women... are valueless and obtain value only by relating to or bonding with men" and "women are 'natural' enemies" (43).

While Lochhead's *Medea* resists such patterns through the Chorus's already mentioned positive attitude toward the ending of marriage, Euripides' *Medea* reflects a search for reconciliation in Medea and Jason's marriage. Similarly, in *Medea* Euripides displays the male-imposed idea that women can only be rivals by not representing Jason's wife Glauke speaking with with Medea. However Lochhead's play challenges that in its representation of the conversation quoted below:

> GLAUKE
> Medea my lady
> I think it's daft we should fight like this
> over a man I am Glauke –
>
> MEDEA
> I've heard of you well my girlie Glauke
> what should we fight for instead? (23)

Despite Medea's insults, the following lines indicate that Glauke tries to keep the peaceful tone of their conversation:

> ... I did not plan it
> I never wanted my happiness should hurt another woman
> do you know how much it hurts me
> my happiness should hurt another woman? (24)

Besides, unlike Medea and similar to the chorus, Glauke challenges the internalization of patriarchy not only by trying to break the myth of female rivalry but also by calling on Medea to show self-respect:

> but if a man no longer loved me wanted freedom
> he could have it
> I'd be too proud to try and keep him. (24)

However Glauke's positive attitude changes as Medea insults her and she also becomes guarded, echoing the stereotypical portrayal of women:

> GLAUKE
> your womb is a dried up pod
> rattling with shrivelled old seeds
> you cannot give him any more babies
> and my sweet firstborn
> already is kicking in mine (26)

In this respect Lochhead offers a realistic representation of the conditions of contemporary women who, according to bell hooks, cannot unite their powers being entrapped by the internalized codes of patriarchy (43-44). However Lochhead attempts to stage "sisterhood" and idealizes it through the feminist sense she foregrounds in the unity of her "CHORUS OF WOMEN of all times, all ages, classes and professions" (7). Lochhead's presentation of female solidarity through the Chorus is reminiscent of that of the American novelist Charlotte Perkins Gilman in *Herland*, a feminist utopia. Through the gazes of three male adventurers travelling to the all-female land, Perkins's novel asserts that in a society not governed by patriarchy, women would have no motivation to fight, but would live in "a peaceful, harmonious sisterhood" (8).

Lochhead's representation of Medea in relation to Jason may be considered stereotypical which in turn reinforces Lochhead's strategy to show Medea as a victim of the patriarchal society. Medea's behaviour foregrounds the significance of her husband's betrayal. Although she utters:

> maybe Jason is not worth it
> this pain this pain (22),

she cannot help looking for revenge. Stereotypically her passion for revenge is fed by her "love for Jason," a love she is ever "stuck with" (23), and is reinforced by the presence of another woman. Medea's following address to Glauke implies a very typical "womanly" challenge:

> indeed I tell you
> take it as a friendly warning
> in the man and wife sense of things
> between Jason and I [sic]
> things have not begun. (26)

However, Medea also reflects some qualities which mainstream feminism likes in women such as a neglect of male gallantries and a resistance towards gender oppression. Euripides' Medea also has a rebellious soul as she resisted the two oppressive male figures Creon and Jason about their decisions on her exile and marriage, respectively. However she has to adopt the role of strategist as she cannot make a direct challenge. For instance in the following lines she implies to Jason that she will eventually take her revenge:

> Go get married. The gods will see to it
> your marriage will change into one of those
> which makes you wish you'd turned it down. (l 746-748)

Such indirect resistance involves hypocrisy which is quite disliked by mainstream feminism. Similarly, she refuses Jason's offer of help, not in order to declare that she can stand alone but because she is offended by him:

> I'll accept no assistance from your friends,
> nor anything from you. Don't make the offer.
> Gifts from a worthless man are without value. (l 735-737)

As for Lochhead's Medea, it may be suggested that she performs well in the tasks mainstream feminism assigns to women. In the following lines Lochhead's Medea refuses Jason's offer which echoes the feminist terminology of positive discrimination directed toward women:

> protection? poisoned prosperity?
> I want no part of it. (20)

Besides, in her address to Jason Lochhead's Medea reveals her intention to make them pay back:

> ...get married man
> your honeymoon will end in bitter tears. (22)

Similarly, in the following lines Lochhead's play makes Medea announce her strategy as instrumental:

> can I convince myself to
> play the part of one of you until I learn it?
> can I get philosophy? sigh and say
> 'it happens' 'I'm not the first and I won't be the last'
> 'in one hundred years it will be all the same'? (23)

Lochhead's Medea cannot act as a stereotypical woman who has internalized patriarchy. Hence she has to answer the next question she poses, "can I wear the mask of moderation" (23), positively and "play[s] the part of one of [them]" instead of really becoming one of them.

Besides, Lochhead's representation of Medea's victimization of her own children is reinforced by the motivation to protect her children from being victims of the patriarchal system. In this respect it may be suggested that Lochhead's play justifies Medea's revenge in a feminist context, quite reminiscent of Toni Morrison's treatment of black female oppression in her novel *Beloved*. In *Beloved*, Sethe, an ex-slave raped by her master, kills her youngest daughter, Beloved, to prevent the repetition of her mother's destiny. The feminist critic Carole Boyce Davies suggests that Morrison's novel "challenge[s] the viciousness of oppression" by offering Sethe's "resistance... at a very personal level" (141, 142). Davies's argument may be related to Lochhead's suggested justification of Medea by representing her stereotypically as a trope of female gender oppression and thus resentment. Given this context, Medea's victimization of her own children may also be considered a sign of individual "resistance" to patriarchy.

Liz Lochhead's *Medea* involves a deconstructive attitude towards the patriarchal themes and patterns embedded in Euripides' *Medea*. By challenging the codes and stereotypes that signify gender oppression, Lochhead's play revisits *Medea* from a feminist perspective. Lochhead's feminism in *Medea* can be related to mainstream feminism which endeavors to unite women with different socio-economic backgrounds against male oppression. Yet as the feminists of color, bell hooks and Gayatri C. Spivak, suggest, mainstream feminism does not deal with ethnic and racial oppression (12-17;168). Their argument can be supported with references to Lochhead's *Medea* which reflects white or mainstream feminism by providing a "*CHORUS OF WOMEN of all times, all ages, classes and professions*" (7) but does not specifically include women of color.

In *Thebans*, Lochhead takes a similar perspective as she revisits *The Theban Plays* by Sophocles and *Phoenician Women* by Euripides in a feminist context. Altering their patriarchal gazes, *Thebans* retells the stories of the two Theban myths in two different parts, *Oedipus* and *Jocasta/ Antigone*.

In Part 1, *Thebans* follows the plot of Sophocles' play but rewrites the dialogues, incorporating its own female focus. For instance, in Sophocles' version, Oedipus's solving of the Sphinx's riddle is foregrounded in an epic manner while the female monster Sphinx is mentioned simply as "the vile enchantress." The following lines from the Priest's address to Oedipus will support this idea:

> It was you, we remember, a newcomer to Cadmus' town,
> That broke our bondage to the vile Enchantress.
> With no foreknowledge or hint that we could give,
> But, as we truly believe, with the help of God,
> You gave us back our life. (Sophocles 26)

Lochhead's version involves a long description of the Sphinx's challenge, quoted below:

> CHORUS
> ...
> ..we come to you because you are not a god
> Oedipus but a man Oedipus
> Oedipus our King our liberator
> the man who freed us
> who by man made logic or divine inspiration
> banished from Theban gates the Sphinx
> our scourge the Sphinx
> who would have killed us all
>
> the Sphinx who devoured us despised us
> whose great wings beat
> whose lion-claws slashed and slit savaged
> who pounced blotting out the sky above us
> whose tail whipped trailing pestilence
> who cackled hatred at us mocking
> her cruel lovely woman's mouth laughing
> you answered her riddle
> you outwitted her (Lochhead 4)

The above lines offer not only a full description of the "great wing[ed]" and "lion-claw[ed]"Sphinx but also an epic-like presentation of her strong challenge to the people of Thebes by "blotting out the sky above [them]" and by "whipp[ing] trailing pestilence" with her tail. By rewriting the female monster Sphinx, Lochhead not only foregrounds the female presence in her play but also calls the reader/audience's attention to one of the earliest stereotypical representations of women as the "Enchantress" (Sophocles 26) as well as the chaotic or ambiguous.

Moreover from an ironic stance, Lochhead reduces the myth of Oedipus and Sphinx to a story of men's search for power both over and through women. As the quote on page 157 sets forth, Lochhead asserts that Oedipus is "a man" who "by man made logic" "outwitted" the Sphinx who is given female qualities with "her cruel lovely woman's mouth laughing" (Lochhead 4). Lochhead further accounts for this "man-made logic" simply as "answer[ing] her riddle" (4). By announcing that Oedipus is "not a god […] but a man" (Lochhead 4), Lochhead also decentralizes the epic qualities Sophocles' play attributes to Oedipus by calling him "great and glorious," "greatest of men" and by asserting that Oedipus can find "any way that god or man can show." (Sophocles 26).

Lochhead's version alters Sophocles' plot by incorporating some parts of Euripides' *Phoenician Women* and thus by foregrounding Jocasta. Jocasta who is represented only in a few short scenes in "Oedipus The King" and whose suicide the reader/audience learns through the conversation between the Attendant and the Chorus, becomes a significant character in both parts of *Thebans*.

In Part 1, Lochhead rewrites Jocasta's lines by truly accommodating her feelings as a woman and a mother. For instance in her scene with Oedipus and Creon, Lochhead's Jocasta utters the following sentimental lines as she tells the story about their baby son whose murder King Laius ordered in fear of the prophecy:

> we had a son
> Laius ripped him
> not three days old yet ripped him from my
> breast
>
> oh I love him still as if it was yesterday
>
> my husband Laius ripped my baby from my breast
> pinned his ankles together and abandoned him
> out on the open moor to die
> I wept tears and milk- ... (Lochhead 16)

Her choice of words, especially in the lines "Laius ripped him ... ripped him from my breast," evokes a similar scene in *The Color Purple* in which Celie, whose stepfather (also the father of her children) has taken her baby away, tells God: "He took it. He took it while I was sleeping [...] He took my other little baby, a boy this time." (Walker 3, 4) Celie's words reflect the same sense of helplessness that Lochhead's Jocasta feels while her baby is being taken away by its father. In both texts the fathers of the babies signify the male authority which oppresses both women and their children. Lochhead's Jocasta also projects the pain of her body, in, "I wept in tears and milk" (16), as does Celie: "I got breasts full of milk running down myself" (Walker 4). The feminist theorist offers a "problematize[ation of] textual references to 'milk' as a signifier for motherhood, breast-feeding as containment for women" since such a conception of milk offers the female body as an object of another subject (Davies 144). Lochhead and Walker respond to Davies's call in their alternative representations of milk as a signifier of futility in the loss and absence of the children. As the feminist theorist suggests, women in a "sexist society" are exposed to " male objectification and dehumanization" (hooks 148, 149). In this respect it may be suggested that Lochhead's *Thebans* adheres to the feminist tradition in terms of both transcribing the experience of female body as an "object" of the male oppressor and centralizing the female perspective as an alternative.

As for Sophocles' version, even Jocasta's motherly feelings for her baby son are left unrepresented. The following quote from Sophocles' play further implies Jocasta's reconciliation with the destiny of her son:

> Jocasta: As for the child,
> It was not yet three days old, when he cast it out
> (By other hands, not his) with riveted ankles
> To perish on the empty mountain-side. (Sophocles 45)

In Jocasta's lines, there is no trace of any regret which implies her internalization of the given order. The only line which involves a little pity is as follows:

> Jocasta: .
>
> For Loxias said a child of mine should kill him.
> It was not to be; poor child, it was he that died.
> (Sophocles 49)

As Jocasta refers to her son from a distance as "poor child," she owns the perspective of an outsider. In other words, Sophocles' Jocasta conforms to the norms of the patriarchal society which, according to the feminist critics, view the female subject always "in relation to the Other's gaze" (Freedman 61).[2] Similarly, Sue-Ellen Case considers "the notion of the female derived from the male point of

---

[2] Given the context of the quote, the term Other should be taken in the Lacanian sense.

view [...] alien" to women themselves since it "reflected the perspective of the gendered opposite" (11). In this respect, as Jocasta, the female subject, internalizes the patriarchal system or owns "the Other's gaze" or "the perspective of the gendered opposite," she gradually becomes her own outsider or Other, "alien" to her own individual experience as a woman.

Part 2 of Lochhead's play focuses on the three female characters, Jocasta and her daughters Antigone and Ismene. The play which is called "Antigone" in Sophocles' version is alternated as "Jocasta/Antigone." which in turn recentralizes Jocasta. Reminiscent of the first scene of *Phoenician Women* by Euripides, Jocasta is still alive in the second part of Lochhead's play and makes the first address to the reader/audience by telling the story of Oedipus from her own perspective.

Jocasta's story strongly reflects a female gaze, focusing on her unhappy marriage with King Laius:

> Jocasta:
>
> married to old man Laius when I was
> hardly older than a child myself this child here
> had no children to him
> though nightly he battered
>
> at the door of my small shut womb
> *a barren union*
> which maddened King Liaus
> that what every slave or slut could get
> unwanted he could not have (Lochhead 33),

It also focuses on her motherly concern for her children which, despite her shame, kept her away from the idea of suicide:

> Jocasta:
>
> When the gods' cruel jest showed itself in all its
> horror
> my shamed husband-son struck out his eyes
> with spike
> with the pins of the brooches that fastened my
> clothes and that he'd
> so often undone but
> I was denied the luxury of extravagant gesture
> do you not think I wished to die?
> I did

> I did
> but I did not
> could not
> I had four helpless children
> two little girls Antigone and Ismene
> her father's pet he named her
> and two fine sons Eteocles and his Mother's
> own big strong Polyneikes
> I was their mother so I could not die (Lochhead 34).

Even suicide is a "luxury" for a mother, since the roles assigned to motherhood already require an individual self-sacrifice. As for the father, any "extravagant gesture" to protect the private self such as Oedipus's blinding himself would be socially acceptable. As mentioned at the beginning of this chapter, the feminist critic Sue-Ellen Case notes that women are oppressed in the "invisible private sphere" while men have the priviledge of attending the "public life" (6). Case's argument may be related to Lochhead's representation of men in search of their places in public in contrast to women who try to preserve their private relationships. For instance, Lochhead's Jocasta is depicted in a search for reconciliation between her two sons, Eteocles and Polyneikes, within the ongoing system; hoping that she can prevent further oppression of her family:

> gods reconcile them unless you think it's fair
> the same mortals should always be the ones to
> suffer? (35)

In other words, men's obsession with power is the source of all their suffering:

> kingship
> power
> who'd want them?
> don't mistake them for happiness?
> an illusion power
> when they see men suckered by it
> the gods start laughing. (Lochhead 44)

The above lines can also be related to Lauis's and Oedipus's former search for power which conventionally serve as their tragic flaws and thus lead to their destruction. If Lauis had not been obssessed with his son's future rivalry and if Oedipus had not challenged Lauis at the crossroads, these tragic incidents would not have taken place. Similarly while asking for the burial of her brother, Antigone wants to protect her family, in turn her private self. However Creon's decision is based on protecting the government, which signifies his public self. Besides, in all cases men are the agents of these actions, women are the ones influenced by their actions. Jocasta, Antigone and Ismene suffer because of decisions made by men; reinforcing the feminist arguments that suggest women's position in patriarchal cultures as "objects"of men (hooks 148). In this respect, Antigone, with her final choice of death, may be considered the only female agent since, although she is entrapped by the dilemma Creon offers, she acts with her free will, against the figure of patriarchal authority .

Lochhead's *Jocasta/Antigone,* Part 2 of *Thebans*, may be considered a challenge to these patriarchal power structures since it offers their decentralization through the female gaze and a replacement of the cultural codes of oppression with nature's codes for peace and harmony. The following quote from Jocasta's address to her two sons centralizes the binary opposite of culture, namely nature, which has traditionally been women's ally as a sign of reconciliation:

>the night-time and the sun each seize the day
>but share it!
>neither one is jealous of the other
>quibbles when it's ousted
>just bides its time and trusts
>the natural cycle will return to its proper place
>central to the tides and in the heavens
>holding sway
>night and day that's you two-
>but you're *more* different. (44)

As the above quote announces the two brothers are "*more* different" than night and day, it addresses the brothers as Others of both each other and nature. If both brothers signify codes of culture, they are already fighting for a losing cause. Furthermore, "cycle," which implies the shifting of power, is addressed as the law of nature. Since from the female gaze power is decentralized and asserted to be arbitrary, the patriarchal codes and stereotypes are deconstructed.

Lochhead's play challenges gender oppression also by centralizing the united power of female bondage. As she chooses to die after her rebellion against Creon, Lochhead's Antigone initially recalls the poison her mother prepared for herself and her two daughters to drink "together […] if Polyneikes won" (79). That they would act together signifies female solidarity. On the other hand, the fact that these women's choices of life or death is bound to the act of other subjects, men, underlines patriarchy's oppression of women by , conventionally, situating them not as decision-makers but as decision-shapers. Going toward her death, Antigone recalls her conversation with her sister, Ismene, which in adherence to the before mentioned feminist call, foregrounds the significance of sisterhood:

> Ismene came said *sister*
> *get up it is your wedding day*
>
> I said *Ismene I know what day it is*
> *today at last the battle*
> *death already has in its greedy maws so many*
>
> Ismene said *yes many*
> *Many will die today Antigone*
> *but it might not be you might not be me*
>
> *get up your lovely wedding dress*
> *we must get it ready.* (79)

Unlike the Sophoclean play, Lochhead's version also gives room to Ismene by representing her feelings after her sister's death. Given the last lines before the Chorus's closure, Lochhead's Ismene announces Lochhead's response to the feminist call for a female solidarity:

> here stands Ismene
> sister of Antigone
> in a sea of death condemned to life. (87)

The above quote also celebrates a female heritage as Ismene is recalled not through her paternal ties but unconventionally through the maternal ones. In other words, Lochhead's *Thebans* rewrites *The Theban Plays* by Sophocles from a feminist perspective, revisiting and revising its implications of gender oppression.

Adhering to the mainstream feminist call, Lochhead's plays operate by deconstructing scenes and codes of gender oppression which the classical plays host; and reconstructing these scenes and codes to liberate women. In other words, in both *Medea* and *Thebans*, Lochhead makes a call for recognition and reconsideration of codes and stereotypes of gender oppression, accommodated in classical representations of women. The structures of these two plays also reinforce their feminist content, which is further studied in 6.3.

6.2. Moraga's Colored and Lesbian Feminism in *Hungry Woman:A Mexican Medea* and *Heart of the Earth: A Popul Vuh Story*

The two plays by Cherrie L. Moraga reflect a strong "radical" feminist voice besides an explicit postcolonial concern which is discussed in Chapter 5. In both plays, Moraga differs from the "mainstream" feminists by foregrounding her colored and lesbian feminism in her challenge to myths of gender oppression.

> We are the colored in a white feminist movement.
> We are the feminists among the people of our culture.
> We are often the lesbians among the straight.
> We do this bridging by naming ourselves and by telling
> our stories in our own words. (Anzaldua, Moraga 23)

The above lines, taken from *This Bridge Called My Back: Writings by Radical Women of Color*, assert Moraga's "difference" from "white" mainstream feminism in telling her own story in her own language.

The above quote may also be related to Moraga's interest in telling her own story of a colored and lesbian Medea. Moraga rewrites Euripides' *Medea* in a feminist context, deconstructing its patriarchal and heterosexual codes. Moraga initially challenges the following stereotypical representation of Medea as a woman betrayed by her husband:

> NURSE:
> And poor Medea is slighted, and cries aloud on the
> Vows they made to each other, the right hands clasped
> In eternal promise. She calls upon the gods to witness
> What sort of return Jason has made to her love.
> She lies without food and gives herself up to suffering,
> Wasting away every moment of the day in tears.
> (Euripides 9-10)

The Nurse's above reference to Medea implies pity directed to Medea, especially because she tortures her body by not eating and continually crying. The last line further announces Medea's disregard of her female body as a source of joy. Female appetite is often related to a desire for sexuality:

> When women are positively depicted as voracious
> about food, ... their hunger for food is employed
> solely as a metaphor for sexual apetite... for example,
> the heroine's unrestrained delight in eating operates as

> sexual foreplay, a way of prefiguring the abandon that
> will shortly be expressed in bed. (Bordo 110)

Based on the above quoted suggestion by Bordo, Medea's diet may be related to her abandonment of sexuality, reflecting a stereotypical portrayal of widowed women . Challenging the conventional repression of female sexuality, Moraga introduces Medea, a Chicana warrior (6), in a lesbian relationship with Luna, an indigenous female warrior. Moraga explicitly represents Medea's sexual desire for Luna; "How do I live now without her breasts? I can't open my mouth to suck her. Luna...?" (11), as well as her desire for oatmeal:

> MEDEA: I like avena.
> NURSE: Avena.
> MEDEA: Oatmeal. It sticks to your ribs, like that commercial.
> (Singing a little jingle) "Sticks to your ribs all day." (11)

Moraga's play reflects her colored lesbian feminism which , in her essay entitled "Queer Aztlan: The Re-formation of Chicano Tribe," she announces as an instrument for the sexual "decolonization" of the indigenous female body:

> Chicanos are an occupied nation within a nation, and women
> and women's sexuality are occupied within the Chicano nation.
> If women's bodies and those of men and women who transgress
> their gender roles have been historically regarded as territories to
> be conquered, they are also territories to be liberated. Feminism
> has taught us this. The nationalism I seek is one that decolonizes
> the brown and female body as it decolonizes the brown and
> female earth. (150)

The above statement refers both to the colonial experience of Chicano(a)s and to the female oppression within the culture; indicating that the Chicanas are exposed to both colonial and gender oppression. It also manifests Moraga's understanding of women of color feminism which views postcolonialism and feminism as interconnected by making a call for a unified Chicano national movement to thoroughly "decolonize" Aztlan.

The play adheres to Moraga's above quoted suggestion by representing the "decoloniz[ation of] the brown and female body" by reconquering Aztlan on a mythical layer. The play proceeds by juxtaposing Medea and Jason or Luna and Chac-Mool as self and Other, foregrounding their engendered and sexual differences. Jason and Chac-Mool are represented as priviledged male subjects who can enter Aztlan. As for Medea, she is on exile in "[a] prison psychiatric hospital in borderlands" (10). Similar to Medea, with her indigenous, female, lesbian identities, Luna signifies "the forbidden inhabitants of the borderland" or *los atravesados*, which Gloria Anzaldua defines as "those who cross over, pass over, or go through the confines of the 'normal'" (25). Thus Luna can not cross the border even if she answers the question the Border Guard poses; "Do you desire—" as "There was no passion there...We slept as sisters..." (62). Similarly, Medea has to have sex with Jason so that she can go back to Aztlan. In other words, the two women have to prove that they are "normal" so as to enter Aztlan. Moraga's incorporation of two indigenous female myths in her version of *Medea,* greatly contributes to her celebration of a colored lesbianism by dethroning the male conception of Aztlan. The Meso-American myth which tells the story of the moon goddess mutilated by her brother, the sun god, announces gender oppression as well as the myth of La Llorona which tells the story of an ever-hungry woman tortured by the male spirits who want to get rid of her unsatisfied desire for food. In her Foreword entitled "Hungry for God," Moraga accounts for her socio-political motivation for revisiting the above mentioned myths:

> *Who are my gods? Who are my people?* The response
> is the same for both questions, I discovered, when I
> discovered the mutilated daughters of our indigenous
> American history of story: La Llorona, Coyolxauhqui,
> Coatlicue. I worship them in my attempt to portray them
> in all their locura, because I admire the living expression
> of their hungers... (x)

The play incorporates the Aztec myth of the moon goddess, mentioned in Chapter 5, into its rewriting of *Medea* by introducing the character Luna, original to Moraga's play. Luna verbally signifies the Spanish word for moon and her frequent depiction in blue may be traced to the conventional association of blue moon with the queer. Moreover it is through Luna that Moraga successfully incorporates the moon goddess Coyolxauhqui's betrayal and victimization by her own brother, which announces male oppression. The play also offers direct references to the myth at the beginning of Act II, as the stage directions initially announce "the stone image of Coatlicue becomes illuminated" and further note "[Luna appears as COYOLXAUHQUI]" (55), accompanied by "pre-Columbian Meso-American music on the background. This scene is related to the last scene of Act I in which

Medea and Jason start to make love, since Coyolxauhqui asserts: "You betrayed me, Madre [Mother]" (55) and Coyolxauhqui's dismemberment by the Aztec sun-god Huitzilopotchli is enacted by Luna and Chac-Mool (Medea's 13-year-old son).

Given this context, Medea may be identified with Coatlicue, Aztec Goddess of Creation and Destruction, also called "the Serpent goddess," who in Mesoamerican myths signifies "fertility" and "earth" (Anzaldua 49). Gloria Anzaldua notes that before Aztecs accepted patriarchy, "the principle of balanced opposition between the sexes existed," through the Lord and Lady of Duality (53-54) the two deities representing the dual forces of nature, as mentioned in Chapter 4. Anzaldua further suggests, "[b]efore the change to male dominance, *Coatlicue*, Lady of the Serpent Skirt, contained and balanced the dualities of male and female, light and dark, life and death" (54). Given this context, Coatlicue possibly stands for a transition to the male order as she unintentionally sacrifices her daughter to the male order by giving birth to a son. Similarly, Moraga's Medea sacrifices her lesbian relationship with Luna to heterosexuality, by having unexpected intercourse with Jason. In this respect, *Hungry Woman: A Mexican Medea* possibly represents the initiation of the male order by Huitzilopochtli's mutilation of Coyolxauhqui and challenges it by offering its lesbian feminist reenactment. In her interview, Moraga asserts her feminist intentions in representing the codes of gender oppression in this Mesoamerican myth .".. as the play *Hungry Woman* says, my god is the mutilated daughter La Luna because she rebelled against the brother" (2006:140). The above lines by Moraga are quite affirmative in tone and they strongly indicate a political discourse on both revisiting the past and resisting it. In her Foreword, Moraga explicitly states that "[she] write[s] to remember— [ ] —because [she] fear[s] that [she] will die before any revolution is born [...] [she] write[s] to imagine, which is a way of remembering, [...] that "we (women) were not always fallen from the mountain." (x) The reference to a future revolution may be related to Moraga's latter statement in her Foreword: "*Imagine freedom*, I tell myself. *Write freedom*," which implies a call for freedom and in turn a revolution.

Another indigenous myth employed in the play is the Aztec myth of La Llorona, the Hungry Woman, after which Moraga names her play. La Llorona also displays gender oppression as it deals with the victimization of "a woman who cried constantly for food" by the male spirits which wanted her to be exiled because she is different: "She can't eat here," "She will have to live somewhere else" (Bierhost 23-25). According to the legend, the hungry woman has mouths everywhere; "in her wrists, ... in her elbows, and ... in her ankles and knees" (Bierhost 23), which signifies her ever-lasting desire for food. To get rid of her, the spirits initially "dragged her down the water" and later "[c]atching her hands and feet, they squeezed her from all directions pushing so hard that she snapped in half at the waist," which the spirits used to make the sky (24). Seeing that the Hungry Woman was still alive, they continued physical violence by making grass and flowers out of her skin; forests from her hair, pools and springs from her eyes, mountains from her shoulders, and valleys from her nose (24, 25). No matter how hard the spirits tried, the hungry woman was still not satisfied; her mouths all around her body. The following quote from Bierhost's narration implies that the cycle of nature always helped her to survive: "When it rains, she drinks. When flowers shrivel, when trees fall, or when someone dies, she eats" (25). Yet the hungry woman is never satisfied, and "[s]ometimes at night, when the wind blows, you can [still] hear her crying for food" (25). Moraga traces this myth to her lesbian feminism as the Cihuatateo foreground the cry of La Llorona just after the conversation between Medea and Luna concerning Medea's son. Medea's son, Chac-Mool, possibly signifies both Medea's betrayal of Luna and Medea's patriarchal ties. The conversation quoted below indicates that although Medea still yearns for Luna, Medea's lesbian love and her love of Aztlan are interrelated;

> MEDEA: (Softening) I had a dream.
> LUNA: Good.
> MEDEA: I dreamed our land returned to us.
> LUNA: Go on.
> MEDEA: You were there. It was the most natural evolution in the world to move from the love of country to love of you.
> This is true even though she had to leave Luna for Jason:
> LUNA: And-
> MEDEA: There was a road of yellow dust, saguaro and maguey. You were laying down the cactus stones one by one to my door.
> LUNA: Why did you shut the door, Medea?
> MEDEA: My son.
> LUNA: No. The truth.
> MEDEA: My son. (80-81)

It may be suggested that Chac-Mool, who ties Medea to Jason, stands in turn for the male aspect of Aztlan, which is patriarchy. As Luna tells the Border Guard, Medea was exiled for her lesbian love (65) and as Jason further notes, "Medea was never to return to Aztlan" (65). Similarly at the end of the above-quoted conversation Medea asserts that Luna is the reason for her exile: "I sacrificed Aztlan for you!" (81).

In this respect loving Luna requires exile while loving Jason implies free entrance to Aztlan. Meral Çileli suggests that "the cultural attributions of gender roles institutionalize men's dominance over women [and] prevent alternatives from gaining cultural definition and recognition" (68). Standing for the "alter-natives" of conventional gender roles, Luna and Medea are neither defined nor recognized by the existing conventions. They are rather located on the "border," alien to the patriarchal signifiers of Aztlan. On the other hand, heterosexuality which according to the lesbian feminists is a reinforcer of "male-defined" system (Allen 35), is the only valid ticket to Aztlan. Given this context, Aztlan stands for the male order itself. As the below quote sets forth, Aztlan is no longer a female territory:

> LUNA: Aztlan was uninhabitable. (81)

Sleeping with Jason whom she had betrayed with Luna, Medea prefers Chac-Mool and Jason to Luna or the patriarchal and heterosexual reality of Aztlan to its lesbian feminist mythology. As the Cihuatateo foreground the image of La Llorona's white veil through which "[t]hey encircle Medea" (63), the play metaphorically represents Medea's ties to the patriarchal and heterosexual face of Aztlan. In this respect the "veil" which in a feminist context signifies women's physical oppression under the patriarchy (Davies 3), can be read as a sign of Medea's heterosexual past which relates her to the patriarchal aspect of Aztlan and leads to her betrayal of La Llorona who symbolizes the female suffering under the patriarchy.

The "veil" also implies a direct reference to the Euripidean play in which it is used by Medea to poison Glauke for being an instrument of Jason's betrayal. Given the context of Moraga's play and the myth of La Llorona, it may be suggested that La Llorona uses the veil to poison Medea who sacrificed Luna to patriarchy:

> LUNA: I don't know what's going on with you. It's like the thought of losing Chac... no kid between us... and we got nothing to disguise what we are to each other. Maybe for you, Chac-Mool makes us less lesbian.
> MEDEA: I'm not you, Luna. I wasn't born that way, the way you like to brag. I'm just a woman worried about keeping her son. You act so damn free. You're not free. (48)

Medea's murder of her son, Chac-Mool, who in the given context signifies the patriarchy, may be related to a female regaining of Aztlan. Unlike the Euripidean Medea, Moraga's Medea is motivated by her son's betrayal of her by becoming a man and preferring to live with his father:

> CHAC-MOOL: I gotta get outta here. I can't do this no more, Mom. I'm just a kid, it's not normal!
>
> MEDEA: You want normal? Then go with your father. He's perfectly normal. It's normal to send your five-year-old child and his mother into exile and then seven years later come back to collect the kid like a piece of property. It's normal for a nearly sixty-year-old Mexican man to marry a teenager. It's normal to lie about your race, your class, your origins, create a completely unoriginal fiction about yourself and then name yourself la patria's poet. But that's normal for a country that robs land from its daughters to give it to its sons unless of course they turn out to be jotos. (74, 75)

As Chac-Mool starts to talk about the "norm," he can no longer live among "the forbidden inhabitants of the borderland" or *los atravesados* in Anzaldua's phrase (25). In other words, Chac-Mool has become a man, as Medea resents realizing:

> [...she addresses Coatlicue]
> MEDEA: Can you smell it, Madre? Mi hijo's manhood.
> He wears it in his sleep now. In the morning I find it in
> a heap on the floor, crumpled in his pijamas. Like Luna,
> I bring the soft flannel to my nose. I inhale. No baby smell.
> No boy. A man moving inside his body. I felt a small rise
> against my thigh just now, a small beating heart hardening
> against that place which was his home. Where's my baby's
> sweet softness now? (90)

Drawing on the play's above-suggested dialogue with the myth of Coatlicue, Medea's murder of her son may also be traced to a deconstruction of the male order which to Anzaldua starts with the story of Coatlicue (54). Moraga's play also blames Coatlicue, whom she calls "Mother," for starting the male order by not acting against her son who oppresses her daughter:

> MEDEA: You betrayed us, Madre Coatlicue.
> You anciana, you who birthed the God of War
>
> Huitziolopotchli.
> His Aztec name sours on my lips,

> as the name of the son
> of the woman who gave me birth.
>
> My mother did not stop my brother's hand
> from reaching into my virgin bed.
> Nor did you hold back the sword
> that severed your daughter's head.
>
> Coyolxauhqui, diosa de la luna.
> [Her arms stretch out to the full moon.]
> Ahora, she is my god.
> La Luna, la hija rebelled.
>
> Te reachazo, Madre. (92)

Here Moraga depicts Madre Coatlicue quite stereotypically; thus in the name of Madre Coatlicue she possibly addresses all mothers—including Demeter—who indirectly serve the patriarchal system by not protecting their daughters against it. Drawing upon the implications of Medea-Coatlicue and Luna-Coyolxauhqui associations, one may suggest that Moraga further offers the reversal of the myth of Coatlicue, by making Medea choose Luna over Chac-Mool who, given this context, stands for Huitziolopotchli, and thus announces the deconstruction of patriarchy:

> MEDEA: ... [addresses Coatlicue]
> What crime do I commit now, Mama?
> To choose the daughter over the son? (91)

In other words, in *The Hungry Woman: A Mexican Medea*, Moraga not only revisits the non-canonized indigenous myths of gender oppression, while rewriting the Euripidean *Medea*, but also announces her textual deconstruction of patriarchy through a reversal of its mythical initiation.

In *Heart of the Earth* Moraga displays a similar attitude in "remember[ing]" the non-canonized indigenous myths of female oppression. Drawing upon the colored and female association of the brown and fertile "earth", Moraga revisits myths of creation not only from a postcolonial perspective, which is offered in 5.2, but also from a feminist perspective. Challenging the engendered patterns in the Mayan myth of creation, *Popul Vuh*, Moraga revisits the myth by centralizing the female presence there.

Following the episodic structure of Popul Vuh, *Heart of the Earth* initially depicts the god Ixpiyacoc and Cucumatz, the serpent, in their attempts to create the earth and its inhabitants. The goddess, Ixmucane, is also represented as Ixpiyacoc's equal in her efforts to help them while she is more busy with corn-planting, as suggested in Chapter 4, which can be traced to the female regenerative powers of nature. As mentioned in Chapter 5.2, corn plays a significant role in *Heart of the Earth* since it is through the corn test that Ixmucane recognizes her daughter-in-law, Ixquic, also called the Blood Woman and the new generation twins are raised under the protection of the corn field. Given the context of the play, corn-planting can be associated with the female efforts for peace as the two women as mothers, Ixmucane and Ixquic, try to keep their sons busy with the corn,

> IXQUIC: This field is ready for replanting. Treat the earth well and she will reward you with abundance and long-life. Here are your planting sticks (She hands the sticks to LOS GEMELOS) (129),

instead of football:

> IXQUIC:...(To Ixmucane) I fear Hunahpu may have inherited his father's love of sports. (128)

Corn can also be taken as a symbol of rebirth since Ixquic gives birth to the next generation twins in the corn field. (127, 128) In this respect, corn also signifies the female fertility since Ixquic gives birth right after she passes Ixmucane's corn test and fills the barren ground with corn. (127) Football, on the other hand, may be taken as a symbol of manhood and destruction since both generations of twins inevitably become its players and consequently experience a journey to the underworld which may be related to a struggle for power, as discussed in 5.2, as well as a desire to go beyond the female earth. The following lines announce the two sons as the Others of their mother,

> IXQUIC: At times, my sons act as strangers... (136)

reminiscient of Medea's statement, "A stranger has inhabited me, taken possession of my body, disguised himself innocently in the sexless skin of my placenta." (87) Both quotes can be related to the feminist theorist Jeffner Allen's consideration of pregnancy as "the mark" of patriarchy on female bodies:

> Stamped, firmly imprinted on women's bodies, is the emblem that our bodies have been opened to the world of men: the shape of the pregnant woman's stomach. From conception to abortion, acts which are biologically different

> and yet symbolically the same, our stomachs are marked
> MOTHER. (322)

The above quote implies that motherhood is an ambiguous situation since it signifies the "mark" of the Other on female bodies by announcing a heterosexual relationship. The child which is an outcome of this relationship, then, can be traced to a sign of female entrance to patriarchy, which signifies the conventional codes of motherhood. In her autobiographical work *Waiting in the Wings: Towards a Queer Motherhood*, Moraga similarly focuses on the codes of having a child in a part of the patriarchal and heterosexual world while narrating the difficulties of her individual experience in raising her son, Raphael, as a lesbian mother:

> ... buried deep inside me,...., I had maintained the rigid conviction that lesbians (that is, those of us on the more butch side of the spectrum)weren't really women. We were women-lovers, a kind of "third sex" and most definitely not men. So having babies was something real women did, not butch lesbians... We were defenders of women and children, children we could never full call our own. (3)

Moraga's consideration of "children" as not "fully" their mothers' also accounts for Moraga's above depictions of the children as "stranger[s]" to their mothers, especially because they are sons. The following lines Moraga utters in an interview, "mothers give birth to our sons for the sons to betray us" (2006:138) and "[i]n terms of feeling he is going to betray me, which is the theme in the play, I think that's what raising your child under patriarchy is. You worry about your son but you worry about your daughter, too" (137), may be related to the above quote from the play as it draws on the implication that children, especially the sons, who signify patriarchy in the given context, are Others of their mothers. Reinforcing her theoretical suggestion, in both of her plays Moraga asserts that the sons' betrayal of their mothers is inevitable in a patriarchal system, either through an unexpected departure;

> IXQUIC: At times, my sons act as strangers. I fear they are leaving me.
> IXMUCANE: It's natural.
> IXQUIC: The fear? Or their leaving?
> IXMUCANE: Both. Both are as common as this corn, (136)

or by becoming a man:

> MEDEA [addresses Coatlicue]
>
> ...what life do I have to offer my son now?
>
> He refuses my gifts and turns to my enemies
> to make a man of him.
> I cannot relinquish my son to them,
> to walk ease camino triste
> where they will call him
> by his manly name
> and he goes deaf
> to hear it. (88)

In this respect similar to *The Hungry Woman*, *Heart of the Earth* offers a strong feminist perspective on mother and son relationship, again drawing on the myth of Coatlicue. Although the myth of Coatlicue is not directly mentioned in *Heart of the Earth* which adheres to the story of *Popul Vuh*, there are some implications that the myth of Coatlicue is also revisited in the play. Actually the stories of creation which *Popul Vuh* and the myth of Coatlicue offer have several points in common. For instance Coatlicue, the goddess of creation, is often identified with "creation" and "destruction" "light and dark" (Anzaldua 54), similar to Ixquic who is called "Daughter of corn [which signifies regeneration] and light!" (Moraga 127) Another parallelism lies in Ixquic's negative aspect as the Blood woman which signifies destruction and serpentry and thus implies an allusion to the destructive face of the Serpent goddess, Coatlicue. Furthermore, the final scene in which Ixbalanque and Hunahpu, the two sons of Ixquic, also called Los Gemelos or the second generation twins, become the sun and the moon, which is quite reminiscent of the myth of Coatlicue. However there is one noteworthy detail which may be suggested as Moraga's announcement of a "deconstruction" of the original, male-centered story and a "reconstruction" of its female counterpart. In the original *Popul Vuh*, the twins become the sun and the moon while the four hundred boys killed in Xibalba become their attendants in the sky; yet the sky itself is not identified with any of the characters (Part II, Chapter 14). Thus it may be claimed that *Popul Vuh* reflects a male conception of the moon, parallel to its centralization of the boys, adventurers experiencing Xibalba, providing detailed accounts of their struggles there, in Part II. However Moraga's play offers an alternative focus by representing its women of the earth in relation to the soil and the corn, in turn to their womanhood and motherhood. Unlike *Popul Vuh*, *Heart of the Earth* focuses on the details of the formation of the sun and the moon. Moraga's play states that Hunahpu becomes the sun and Ixbalanque becomes the moon, given "la luna's full female face." (152) Furthermore it offers Ixquic as the sky, noting that the mother of the twins "[is] named by la luna's changing aspects." (152) It may, thus, be argued that Moraga's play deconstructs the male dominance in *Popul Vuh* by filling in the above-mentioned gap. One may further suggest that *Heart of the Earth* rewrites the story of *Popul Vuh* through the myth of Coatlicue. Hunahpu's reference to the sliced faces of the moon as "Waning moon. Waxing moon. El lado oscuro de la luna" (152) may be related to a foreshadowing of his future mutilation of Ixbalanque, signifying the story of Huitzilopotchli and Coyolxauhqui. Given this context, it may be suggested that the play represents the times before the dismemberment of the female race to which Gloria Anzaldua refers as times when "the principle of balanced opposition between the sexes existed" (53-54). The representation of the god Ixpiyacoc and Ixmucane as equals also supports the above argument. In this respect, it may be concluded that "Heart of the Earth" writes its own female story of creation through *Popul Vuh* by remembering and transcribing the non-canonized female mythology.

Heart of the Earth also reflects a dialogue with the myth of the hungry woman, La Llorona, which reinforces the play's stance against female oppression. As mentioned in 4.2 and 5.2, the myth of La Llorona tells the story of a hungry woman whose dissatisfaction leads to her physical oppression by the male spirits. *Heart of the Earth* responds to it by its recurrent references to hunger. When Ixpiyacoc, the first generation twins and the Wooden-Man are hungry (111, 116 and 137), they are all fed by the variable meals of corn.Yet the Blood Woman, Ixquic also urges for food, "Must I die of this relentless hunger?" (121) but she is left to starvation by the Lords of Xibalba since "[t]hey want everyone empty and bone-gray like them." (122) Reminiscent of the myth of La Llorona in which the male water spirits cut her womb to stop her fertility which they think is the source of her hunger, the Patriarchal Pus and the Blood Sausage, the two Lords of the Underworld, order her heart to be cut out and brought to them as soon as they realize the pregnancy of the Blood Woman (123).

Thus it may be suggested that in *Heart of the Earth*, too, Moraga draws upon the indigenous myths of Coatlicue and La Llorona as signs of female oppression and challenges them, respectively, by foregrounding her heroine, Ixquic or the

Blood Woman, as the sky and by accommodating her in the ancient Mayan world of gender equality where "the Blue-Green Kukulcan reigns. And Ixmucane and Ixpiyacoc ... love all their children." (122)

6.3. A Comparative Approach to Lochhead and Moraga's Feminist Voices and Structures

Both Liz Lochhead and Cherrie L. Moraga display their feminist stances in their rewritings of myths of oppression. The two women playwrights also share a common ground in both remembering and resisting myths which reflect gender oppression. Yet their plays reflect two different understandings of feminism, which, respectively, go parallel to the individual backgrounds or experiences of Lochhead and Moraga.

In her rewritings of the two Greek plays, Lochhead takes a white European feminist perspective, presented against a Scottish background. As noted in 6.1, she does not ever mention women of color, either in *Medea* or in *Thebans*. Although Lochhead's plays deal with hierarchal and ethnic oppression besides gender oppression, they do not refer to racial oppression which is foregrounded in women of color feminism. Besides, as mentioned in 5.3, Lochhead's plays both resist and adhere to the European contexts of the Greek plays. Similarly, Lochhead's feminist voice in her plays reflects her identity as a white European woman with a Scottish ancestry who challenges the patriarchal codes and gender oppressive signs of her culture.

Moraga, however, offers a postcolonial feminist stance towards oppression. Both *The Hungry Woman* and *Heart of the Earth* manifest her interdependent understanding of ethnic, racial and gender oppression, which is discussed in 5.2 and 6.2. In other words, Moraga's plays represent the multiple times Other'ed women, adhering to women of color feminism. Besides, as mentioned in 6.2, Moraga owns a distinctly Chicana feminist voice in her "rememberance" of engendered Aztec and Mayan myths.

Besides, Lochhead's plays represent female oppression under patriarchy while Moraga's plays deal with gender oppression which has a broader concern as it also involves queer oppression. Another noteworthy distinction between Lochhead's and Moraga's feminism is their different articulations on the female body as heterosexual and lesbian, respectively. Lochhead's plays reflect a heterosexual understanding of feminism which draws upon the liberation of the female body in a sexual relationship with man. Yet, as noted in 6.2, Moraga offers a lesbian feminist perspective in her insights on the thorough "decolonization" of the female body by patriarchy, which also directs her to political activism.

As discussed in 6.1 and 6.2, respectively, Lochhead's *Medea* and *Thebans* make a strong call for a female solidarity against patriarchy and female oppression while Moraga's *The Hungry Woman* and *Heart of the Earth,* under the light of her theoretical scope, urge women to activism. In this respect, Lochhead's white, European, Scottish, heterosexual feminism may be traced to a mainstream, social feminist voice which, to stop female oppression, asks for a revision of gender codes and stereotypes within the given system. On the other hand, Moraga's colored, Mexican-American or Chicana, lesbian feminism may be considered more political and radical as it suggests that it looks for a "revolution." (2003:x) Lochhead and Moraga also challenge the oppressive structures of the Western myths by subverting their patterns. As discussed in Chapter 3, Augusto Boal traces the classical theatre, which adheres to the Aristotelian tradition, to a system of oppression. Boal also offers a model of oppression through which he suggests that the classical theatre operates. Drawing upon Boal's model, the oppressive structures of *Medea* and *The Theban Plays* are examined as well as those of other major Western myths, and it is further suggested that in both tragedies with female protagonists, their *hamartia*s conflict initially with those of the alternative, male, protagonists, and later with the "social ethos," usually with the chorus, in Medea's case also with the Nurse. As the female reader/audience accompanies the female protagonist in her rise and fall, both due to her disobedience to patriarchy, she is made to learn that any radical stance against male rule will lead to tragic consequences of disobedience to male authorities and an internalization of patriarchy is evoked through the Chorus. The adaptation of Boal's model to female oppression in classical representations of women, which is suggested in Chapter 3, may be recalled to better account for Lochhead and Moraga's subversions of them:

> -The disobedience of the female protagonist (hamartia or individuals) to the will of the male authority and the conventions (social ethos)

> -Her initial rise through her disobedience (Medea's disobedience to her own father regarding Jason or Antigone's disobedience to Creon regarding her

brother); witnessed by the reader/audience which leads to empathy and then her fall due to excessive disobedience. Both the female protagonist's and the female reader or audience's recognition of the hamartia

-Purification through her suffering, which in turn leads to Catharsis as the female reader/audience witnesses the tragic outcomes of the hamartia (disobedience to male authority)

As she challenges the female oppression implied in Western myths, Lochhead subverts the above given model in both *Medea* and *Thebans*. Lochhead initially offers an alternative female protagonist (in *Medea*, Glauke; in *Antigone*, Jocasta) which blocks a possible identification with either of the protagonists. Thus she also decentralizes the focus on the hamartias of the male protagonists (Jason and Creon) in their clashes with those of the female ones. For instance what leads Medea to act is not only Jason's but also Glauke's betrayal since in Lochhead's play, "Jason is not worth it" (22). Lochhead may be following a similar strategy in representing Jocasta as still alive in *Jocasta/Antigone* and making her the source of Antigone's motivation to act. Moreover, she offers representations of two different types of female protagonists: the conformist and the nonconformist. While the hamartias of the nonconformists (Medea and Antigone) contradict those of the male protagonists (Jason, Creon and Creon) and the patriarchal social ethos (the Nurse and the Chorus in the original plays), the hamartias of the conformists (Glauke and Jocasta) contradict the feminist social ethos (Lochhead's alternative Nurse and Chorus). On the other hand, as argued in Section 6.1, in both plays Lochhead challenges the conventional signifiers of patriarchy, namely the Nurse and the Chorus, by bonding them to each other and to the protagonists through "female solidarity," a "*CHORUS OF WOMEN of all times, all ages, classes and professions*" (7), and by representing them not as signs of internalized patriarchy but as those of feminist consciousness. In other words, one can suggest that Lochhead's plays operate as follows:

-Female disobedience (Medea, Antigone) to patriarchy (Jason and Creon) and female betrayal (Glauke, Jocasta) of another female (Medea, Antigone) by conforming to the given order.

-The fall of the female protagonist for disobeying the norm which leads to an awareness of female oppression in the reader or audience and the fall of the second female protagonist for betraying her own sex which leads to an awareness of internalized patriarchy.

- Feminist social consciousness is evoked and a call for female solidarity is made.

In this respect, Lochhead's theatre subverts the patriarchal patterns of the Aristotelian tradition of theatre and offers an alternative feminist pattern. Moraga's theatre challenges the above-mentioned patriarchal structures of the Aristotelian tradition in a more radical way. As discussed in 6.2, in *The Hungry Woman* she dethrones the Euripidean play together with its male protagonists Jason and Creon and alters them with indigenous myths with female heroines Luna and the Hungry Woman. Making Medea betray Jason, she announces her reversal rather than the subversion of the Euripidean play as well as her indifference to representing the male hamartia against that of her female protagonist. Medea's betrayal of Luna or her heterosexual tendency which may be considered the reason for her fall, is foregrounded as her only hamartia. Moraga also allocates the role of the Greek Chorus to all female characters (Luna, Medea, Mama Sal, Havannah) who in the play also act as story-tellers, travelers among times and spaces. In other words Moraga disintegrates the voice of "common sense" or patriarchy and incorporates female stories of different times and places from the perspectives of different women, involving the lesbians and women of color. This strategy enables Moraga to make her female protagonists recognize female oppression of all times and all places simultaneously with the reader or audience, which in turn leads to raising of feminist consciousness.

Similarly in *Heart of the Earth,* Moraga offers a Chicana version of an old story of creation. By making the female protagonist fall to the earth because she experienced sexuality which is against the patriarchal norms—"But Father, I have not known a man in the biblical sense"(123)—and making the figure of male authority announce women's oppression in all circumstances—"This is not the bible. This is the *Popol Vuh*" (123)—Moraga asserts that her play challenges the oppression of women in both Genesis and the American indigenous myths of creation. Similar to Medea's fall from Aztlan, which is not a real fall since "Aztlan was [is] uninhabitable" for women (81), Ixquic's fall to the earth is not a real fall but in fact a rise since the pre-creation Mayan world where, "Ixmucane and Ixpiyacoc ... love all their children" (122), is depicted as a better place for women. As noted in 6.2, the play deconstructs the linear structure of conventional theatre and represents the pre-creation Mayan world of gender equality as an alternative to the patriarchal systems of *Popol Vuh* and Genesis. Given the above context, it may be suggested that Moraga, as compared to Lochhead, offers a more revolutionary feminist stance, lesbian and postcolonial, in revisiting myths of gender oppression. To better justify Moraga's reversal of the conventional patterns of "theatre of oppression" which is discussed above, the following process can be suggested:

> - Female betrayal of female (heterosexuality) or female disobedience to patriarchy (experiencing female sexuality).
>
> - Fall for the former, rise for the latter. A Chicana feminist awareness is evoked in the reader/audience as the female characters tell and enact the indigenous myths of female oppression.
>
> -Political consciousness is raised, a feminist revolution is addressed.

7. Conclusion

In this study myths are defined as old stories which reflect and reinforce patterns leading to an acceptable social system while oppression is taken as an excessive use of authority over someone to limit his or her freedom of choice. Furthermore, postcolonial and feminist theories are examined as theory-driven movements against oppression. Parallel to a revision of postcolonial and feminist theories, the canonization of Western and patriarchal myths is noted. Given a postcolonial and feminist context, rewriting—which is the technique used in Liz Lochhead's *Medea* and *Thebans* and in Cherrie L. Moraga's *The Hungry Woman: A Mexican Medea* and *Heart of the Earth: A Popol Vuh Story*—embeds resistance toward ethnic or racial and gender oppression in dramatic form.

With references to the frequently visited myths of the Western canon, especially to Euripides' *Medea* which is rewritten by both Lochhead and Moraga, and Sophocles' *The Theban Plays* which is rewritten by Lochhead, it is argued that Western myths imply hierarchical, ethnic or racial and gender oppression. Drawing upon Augusto Boal's suggestion of a system of oppression in the Aristotelian tradition of theatre which operates through *catharsis* by reinforcing conformity to norms, the patterns of oppression in Western myths are specified. A female-specific adaptation of Boal's model is suggested and exemplified with references to *Medea* and *Antigone,* the two major Greek myths with female protagonists. The above-mentioned model is later related to Lochhead and Moraga's rewritings of myths. Building upon these interpretations, Liz Lochhead and Cherrie L. Moraga's responses to patterns of oppression are further examined as being either repetitive or resistant.

Considering their exclusion from the literature syllabi, as another sign of ethnic oppression, this study also examines the noncanonized Scottish, Celtic and Mayan, Aztec myths which have significant traces in Scottish and Chicana writings, respectively. The Scottish myth, Beira, which accounts for the cycle of seasons and the Mayan myth, Popol Vuh, which tells an alternative story of creation, are foregrounded since they are related to Lochhead and Moraga's rewritings of the classics. It is observed that both Scottish, Celtic and Aztec, Mayan myths deal with nature with different focuses: respectively its cyclical and dual nature. These myths are compared and contrasted with Greek myths which imply not naturally but culturally governed ways of life. The Scottish and Chicana/o traditions of writing are studied in relation to their reflections of oppression while Lochhead and Moraga's original plays (the ones which are not a rewriting of other texts) are examined in relation to their stance against oppression. In this respect Lochhead and Moraga's authentic contributions to their own national canons are foregrounded while their different contributions are related to their different backgrounds and socio-political stances.

Lochhead and Moraga's rewritings of myths of oppression are examined in terms of content and structure. Liz Lochhead and Cherrie L. Moraga not only visit myths of hierarchical, ethnic or racial and gender oppression, but also rewrite them in postcolonial and feminist contexts. In their revisitations of myths of ethnic or racial and gender oppression, Lochhead and Moraga employ distinct voices and authentic styles. The two playwrights not only re-present the old stories of oppression to contemporary minds but also represent a challenge to such oppression in their use of alternative dramatic techniques. Their use of Celtic, Scottish and Aztec, Mayan oral literatures in their rewritings of Greek myths generates dialogue between the less known myths and the mainstream Western canon. While, in *Medea*, Lochhead challenges the Scottish oppression in Britain by foregrounding a Scottish diction as an alternative to standard English, she follows the Euripidean text fairly closely in story and plot. Similarly, in *Thebans*, she repeats the stories of Oedipus and Antigone although in some parts of the play she inserts elements from Sophocles' Theban plays and Euripides' *The Phoenician Women*. Both *Medea* and *Thebans* involve signs of a Scottish background as well. This attitude is considered a sign of Lochhead's in-between position as a Scot and a European. In other words, her subversion of the Greek myths is related to her challenge to the noncanonization of the Scottish myths and legends while her alternation of a Greek story with another Greek one, namely Sophocles' Theban plays and Euripides' *The Phoenician Women*, implies her partial adherence to the European tradition . As for Moraga, it can be stated that both of her rewritings introduce a reversal rather than a subversion of the European myths. By centralizing the indigenous myths of La Llorona, Coatlicue and Popol Vuh as opposed to their European counterparts, Medea and Genesis, Moraga's plays dethrone the Eurocentric myths. Moraga's rewritings of myths also display resistance to the Western tradition in terms of their form by challenging the Aristotelian unities of time, space and subject matter, all at once, in their nonlinear, multispatial and plural-voiced representations. Also, owing to Cherrie L. Moraga's background as a theorist, her challenge announces itself in a more political and revolutionary way. In this respect, this study claims that in revisiting the European myths, Lochhead's attitude in the two plays implies more repetition and remembrance and less resistance compared with Moraga's, which is a result of Lochhead's European identity. On the other hand, Moraga's revolutionary resistance to the European tradition is foregrounded in relation to her colored Chicana indigenism. Lochhead's rewritings are considered "adaptations" in accordance with Lochhead's reference to them, of Greek myths to more liberal contexts and they reinforce the common idea that "myths never die; they just transform," while those of Moraga celebrate their differences and thus respond to the following call by Adrienne Rich: "We need to know the writing of the past, and know it differently than we have ever known it; not to pass on a tradition but to break its hold over us" (35).

Liz Lochhead and Cherrie Moraga share another common ground in their feminist perspectives on myths of oppression. This study also examines Lochhead and Moraga's rewritings of myths in different feminist contexts. While Lochhead's plays echo mainstream feminism with its white heterosexual gaze, Moraga's plays reflect the alternative trends in feminism, namely women of color and lesbian waves. Lochhead and Moraga not only decentralize the patriarchal themes of old stories but also alter their conventional forms, which is already another signifier of hegemony. In *Medea* and *Thebans*, Lochhead challenges the patriarchy by subverting the classical representation of the Greek Chorus as a signifier of internalized conventions. Instead she offers a chorus of women with feminist awareness. Another sign of Lochhead's formally expressed resistance to patriarchal myths of early Europe is her allocation of the role of the female protagonist to alternative female characters. The centralization of the Nurse and the representation of Glauke in *Medea* displace Medea as the only female protagonist. Similarly, in *Thebans*, Part 2, Jocasta and Ismene accompany Antigone, which in turn is related to Lochhead's foregrounding of a female bondage. This study suggests that Moraga's use of dramatic technique also reflects a strong resistance to patriarchal myths by reversing them in story and in plot. Moraga's initial incorporation and further deconstruction of the two indigenous myths of female oppression contribute to her representation of a reverse patriarchy. Moraga's disintegration of the Greek chorus and her involvement instead of female storytellers in *The Hungry Woman*, is considered a sign of her resistance to adopting the gender oppressive patterns of Western representation. Similarly, Moraga's nonlinear and nonprogressive representation of the Mayan creation myth of Popol Vuh in dialogue with Western myths of Genesis, in *Heart of the Earth*, is related to Moraga's "decolonization" (Mayorga 155) of her female text from the male-centered patterns. This study contends that in her rewritings of European myths, Lochhead reflects her European and Scottish identities as she both follows and subverts patterns of oppression. Naming her plays *Medea* and *Thebans*, and calling them "adaptations" (102) of the Greek classics, in Gonzalez's interview, Lochhead displays her adherence to her European heritage. On the other hand, through her engendered and Scottish contexts or by foregrounding the noncanonized , she also resists the codes of oppression the European literary canon hosts. As for Moraga, she remembers the indigenous myths of oppression; and repeats and challenges their structures. This process also leads to Moraga's reversal of the Eurocentric patterns of oppression. What Moraga does is resist the European patterns of oppression without repeating them. Drawing upon the abovementioned analysis, this study claims Lochhead and Moraga's different rewritings are the female-specified version of Boal's model of oppression. According to Boal's model, the Aristotelian tradition of theatre includes systematic oppression through *empathy* and *catharsis*. Boal argues that the former leads to the audience's identification with the protagonist and the latter implies purification through the protagonist's suffering because of his/her tragic flaw or *hamartia*. Boal also suggests that the classical theatre reflects different types of conflicts between *hamartia* and social *ethos* which in turn leads to tragic consequences. In other words, individual deviation from the norm is punished while social conformity is positively reinforced by the Aristotelian tradition of theatre. Drawing on Boal's model of oppression in the Aristotelian tradition, this study suggests that Lochhead and Moraga both authentically challenge these myths of oppression by rewriting not only their oppressive stories but also their oppressive structures.

    This study is intended to contribute to prospective studies on the two contemporary women playwrights, Liz Lochhead and Cherrie L. Moraga. It is also expected that this study will inspire further research on less studied myths so that in the long run, these authentic myths will also be included in literature course syllabi and the literary canon.

Works Cited

Abel, Elizabeth, Barbara Christian, Helene Moglen. Introduction: "The Dream of a Common Language." *Female Subjects In Black and White: Race, Psychoanalysis, Feminism*. Berkeley, Los Angeles, London: U of California P, 1997. Print.

Acheson, James and Romana Hulk, ed. Preface. Introduction. *Contemporary British Poetry: Essays In Theory and Criticism*. New York: State U of New York P, 1996. Print.

Alarcon, Norma and Ana Castillo, Cherrie Moraga, eds. *The Sexuality of Latinas*. Berkeley: Third Woman P, 1993. Print.

--- . "The Theoretical Subject(s) of This Bridge Called My Back and Anglo-American Feminism." *Criticism in the Borderlands: Studies in Chicano Literature, Culture and Ideology*. Eds. Hector Calderon and Jose David Salvidar. Durham and London: Duke UP, 1991. Print.

Alcoff, Linda. "Cultural Feminism versus Poststructuralism: The Identity Crisis in Feminist Theory." *Signs* 13: 3 (1988): 405-436. Print.

Alcott, Louisa May. *Little Women*. Ed. Elaine Showalter. New York: Penguin, 1989. Print.

Anzaldua, Gloria. *Borderlands: La Frontera/The New Mestiza*. San Francisco: Aunt Lute Books, 1999. Print.

Anzaldua, Gloria and Analousie Keating, eds. *this bridge we call home: radical visions for transformation*. New York: Routledge, 2002. Print.

Anzaldua, Gloria and Cherrie L. Moraga, eds. *This Bridge Called My Back: Writings by Radical Women of Color*. Berkeley: Third Woman P, 1984. Print.

Anzaldua, Gloria, ed. *Making Face, Making Soul/Haciendo Caras: Creative and Critical Perspectives by Feminists of Color*, San Francisco: Aunt Lute Books, 1990. Print.

Aristotle. "Poetics." *Aristotle's Poetics*. Ed. O.B. Hardison. Trans. Leon Golden. Eaglewood Cliffs, NJ: Prentice-Hall, 1968. Print.

Arredondo, Gabriela F. (ed) et al. *Chicana Feminisms*. US: Duke UP, 2003. Print.

Arrizon, Alicia. *Latina Performance: Traversing The Stage*. Bloomington: Indiana UP, 1999. Print.

Austen, Jane. *Pride and Prejudice*. Ed. Tony Tanner. Harmondsworth: Penguin, 1972. Print.

---. *Sense and Sensibility*. London: Penguin, 1994. Print.

Barthes, Roland. "The Death of the Author." *Image, Music, Text/Roland Barthes; essays selected and translated by Stephen Heath*. New York: Hill & Wang, 1978. Print.

---. *Elements of Semiology*. Trans. Annette Lavers and Colin Smith. New York: Hill and Wang, 1968. Print.

---. *Empire of Signs*. Trans. Richard Howard. New York: Hill and Wang, 1982. Print.

---. *Mythologies*. Trans. Annette Lavers. New York: The Noonday P, 1972. Print.

---. *The Rustle of Language*. Berkeley: U of California P, 1989. Print.

---. *S/Z*. Trans. Richard Miller. New York: Hill and Wang: The Noonday P, 1974. Print.

Bejarano, Yvonne Yarbro. *The Wounded Heart: Writing on Cherrie Moraga*. Austin: U of Texas P, 2001. Print.

Benston, Kimberly W. *Performing Blackness*. London & New York: Routledge P, 2000. Print.

Bettelheim, Bruno. *Freud and Man's Soul*. London: The Hogarth P, 1983. Print.

Bhabha, Homi K. *The Location of Culture*. London and New York: Routledge, 1994. Print.

Bieber, Margaret. *The History of the Greek and Roman Theatre*. Princeton N.J: Princeton UP, 1939. Print.

Bierhost, John . *The Hungry Woman: Myths and Legends of the Aztecs*. New York: Quill William Morrow P, 1993. Print.

Boal, Augusto. *Ezilenlerin Tiyatrosu*. Çev. Necdet Hasgül. İstanbul: Boğaziçi Üniversitesi Yayınları, 2008. Print.

Bordo, Susan. *Unbearable Weight: Feminism, Western Culture and the Body*. London: U of California P, 1995. Print.

Bronte, Anne. *Agnes Grey*. Harmandsworth: Penguin, 1994. Print.

Bronte, Charlotte. *Jane Eyre*. New York: Barnes & Noble Books, 1992. Print.

Bronte, Emily. *Wuthering Heights*. Oxford: Oxford UP, 1999. Print.

Cabeza de Vaca, Álvar Núñez: *The Narrative of Cabeza De Vaca*. Trans. Rolena Adorno and Patrick Charles Pautz. Lincoln, NE: U of Nebraska P, 2003. Print.

Calderon, Hector and Jose David Salvidar. *Criticism In The Borderlands*. Durham, NC: Duke UP, 1991. Print.

Campbell, Joseph. *The Masks of God: Creative Mythology*. New York: Penguin P, 1991. Print.

--- . *The Power of the Myth*. New York: Anchor Books, 1991. Print.

--- . *The Masks of God: Occidental Mythology*. New York: Penguin, 1964. Print.

Cantu, Norma E. and Olga Najera-Ramirez (eds).*Chicana Traditions: Continuity and Change*. Urbana: U of Illinois P, 2002. Print.

Carr, Marina. *By the Bog of Cats. Plays One*. London: Faber and Faber, 1999. Print.

Carter, Steve. *Pecong*. New York: Broadway P, 1993. Print.

Case, Sue-Ellen. *Feminism and Theatre*. New York: Routledge, 1994. Print.

Castle, Gregory. *The Blackwell Guide to Literary Theory*. Oxford and Malden, MA: Blackwell, 2007. Print.

Cervantes, Miguel de. *Don Quixote*. Hertfordshire: Wordsworth Classics, 1993. Print.

Chaucer, Geoffrey. *Canterbury Tales*. Cambridge; New York: Cambridge UP, 2004. Print.

Çileli, Meral. "Denial of Sexuality and Gender Roles in Lessing's *The Grass is Singing*." *Atenea* XXI: 3. 65-75. Print.

Collins, Patricia Hill. *Black Feminist Thought*. New York and London: Routledge, 1991. Print.

Colop, Sam, ed. *Popol Wuj: versión poética K'iche'..* Quetzaltenango; Guatemala City: Proyecto de Educación Maya Bilingüe Intercultural.Editorial Cholsamaj, 1999. Print.

Datan, Nancy. "After *Oedipus: Lauis, Medea* and Other Parental Myths." *The Journal of Mind and Behavior* 3:1. 17-26. Print.

Davies, Carole Boyce. *Black Women, Writing and Identity: Migrations of the Subject*. London and New York: Routledge, 1994. Print.

De Beauvoir, Simone. *The Second Sex*. Ed. and trans. H.M. Parshley. Harmondsworth: Penguin, 1977. Print.

Defoe, Daniel. *Moll Flanders*. London: Penguin, 1994. Print.

Delphy, Christine. *Close to Home: A Materialist Analysis of Women's Oppression*. Trans. Diana Leonard. Amherst: U of Massachusetts P, 1984. Print.

Derrida, Jacques. *Of Grammatology*. Trans. Gayatri C. Spivak. Baltimore: Johns Hopkins UP, 1976. Print.

Doyle, Sir Canon. *Sherlock Holmes*. Ed. Sidney Paget. New York: Chatham River P, 1983. Print.

Dreyfus, H.L. and Rabinov, P (Ed). *Michael Foucault: Beyond Structuralism and Hermeneutics*. Chicago: U of Chicago P, 1983. Print.

Du Bois, W.E.B. *The Souls of Black Folk*. New York: Dover P, 1994. Print.

Duffy, Carol Ann. *The World's Wife*. London: Picador, 1999. Print.

Eagleton, Terry. *The Idea of Culture*. Oxford and Malden, MA: Blackwell, 2000. Print.

---, ed. *Ideology*. London and New York: Longman, 1994. Print.

---. *Literary Theory: An Introduction*. Minneapolis: U of Minnesota P, 1983. Print.

El Plan Espirituel de Aztlan. Denver, CO: March 1969. Print.

Elam, Keir. *The Semiotics of Theatre and Drama*. Ed.Terence Hawkes. London and NewYork: Methuen, 1980. Print.

Ellis, Peter Berresford. *Celtic Myths and Legends*. Philadelphia and London: Running P, 2008. Print.

Euripides. *Medea*. New York: Dover Thrift P, 1993. Print.

Euripides. "The Phoenecian Women." *Orestes, and other plays*. Ed. Philip Vellacott. Harmondsworth: Penguin, 1972. Print.

Fanon, Frantz. *Black Skin, White Masks*. New York: Grove P, 1967. Print.

---. *The Wretched of the Earth*. Trans. Constance Farrington. Harmondsworth: Penguin, 1967. Print.

Feyder, Linda. *Shattering The Myth: Plays by Hispanic Women*. Houston, Texas: U Texas, 1992. Print.

Firestone, Shulamith. *The Dialectic of Sex: The Case for Feminist Revolution*. Morrow,1970. Print.

Fish, Stanley. "Commentary: The Young and the Restless." *The New Historicism*. Ed. H. Aram Veeser. New York: Routledge, 1989. 303-316. Print.

Flaubert, Gustav. *Madame Bovary*. London: Penguin, 1995. Print.

Foucault, Michel. *The Archeology of Knowledge*. London: Tavistock P, 1972. Print.

---. *Power and Knowledge: Selected Interviews and Other Writings*. Ed. Colin Gordon. Trans. Colin Gordon. New York: Pantheon, 1980. Print.

---. "Truth and Power." *Essential Works of Foucault*. Ed. James D. Faubion. New York: Penguin, 1994. Print.

Freedman, Barbara. "Frame-Up: Feminism, Psychoanalysis, Theatre." *Performing Feminisms: Feminist Critical Theory and Theatre*. Ed. Sue-Ellen Case. Baltimore and London: The Johns Hopkins UP, 1990. 54-76. Print.

Friedan, Betty. *The Feminine Mystique*. New York: Norton, 1963. Print.

Frye, Northrop. "Archetypal Criticism: Theory of Myths." *Twentieth-Century Literary Theory: A Reader*. Ed. K. M. Newton. Hong Kong: MacMillan, 1988. Print.

---. *The Great Code: The Bible and Literature*. New York: Harcourt Brace, 1982. Print.

Gandhi, Leela. *Postcolonial Theory: A Critical Introduction*. Edinburgh: Edinburgh UP, 1998. Print.

Gates, Henry Louis Jr. *The Signifying Monkey . A Theory of Afro-American Literary Criticism*. New York and Oxford: Oxford UP,1988. Print.

---. *Figures in Black: Words, Signs and the "Racial Self."* New York and Oxford: Oxford UP, 1989. Print.

Gilman, Charlotte Perkins. *Herland and Selected Stories*. Ed. Barbara H. Solomon. New York: Signet Classic, 1992. Print.

Gomez-Quinones, Juan. *Chicano Politics: reality and promise, 1940-1990*. Albuquerque: U of New Mexico P, 1990. Print.

Greer, Germaine. *The Female Eunch*. New York: McGraw-Hill, 1971. Print.

Hamilton, Edith. *Mythology: Timeless Tales of Gods and Heroes*. New York and Boston: Warner Books, 1999. Print.

Hardy, Thomas. *Tess of D'urbervilles*. London and New York: Penguin P, 2003. Print.

Hart, Lynda. Introduction. *Making a Spectacle*: *Feminist Essays on Contemporary Women's Theatre*. Michigan: U of Michigan P, 1998. Print.

Hawthorne, Nathaniel. *The Scarlet Letter: A Romance*. Ed. Susan Cockroft.London: Cambridge UP, 1997. Print.

Holdsworth, Nadine and Mary Luckhurst, eds. *A Companion to Contemporary British and Irish Drama*. Oxford: Blackwell, 2007. Print.

Homer. *The Iliad*. Trans. E.V.Rieu. Harmondsworth, Eng: Penguin, 1984. Print.

---. *The Odyssey*. Trans. Albert Cook. New York: Norton, 1967. Print.

hooks, bell. *Ain't I A Woman*: *Black Women and Feminism*. Brooklyn: South End P, 1981. Print.

---. *Feminist Theory: From Margin To Center*. London: Pluto P, 2000. Print.

---. *Talking Back: Thinking Feminist Thinking Black*. Brooklyn: South End P, 1989. Print.

Hutcheon, Linda. *A Theory of Parody: The Teachings of Twentieth-Century Art Forms*. Champaign and Urbana: U of Illinois P, 2001. Print.

---. *Narcissistic Narrative*: *the metafictional paradox*. Waterloo, Ont: Wilfrid Laurier UP, 1980. Print.

Hyde, Lewis. *Trickster Makes This World*. New York: North Point P, 1989. Print.

James, Joy and T. Denean Sharpley-Whiting, ed. *The Black Feminist Reader*. Oxford and Malden, MA: Blackwell, 2000. Print.

Jameson, Fredric. *Postmodernism, or, the Cultural Logic of Late Capitalism*, Durham: Duke University Press, 1991. Print.

Jung, Carl Gustav. *The Archetypes and the Collective Unconscious*. New York: Princeton UP, 1968. Print.

Irigaray, Luce. *The Irigaray Reader*. Ed. Margaret Whitford. Oxford: Blackwell, 1992. Print.

Iser, Wolfgang. "The Reading Process: A Phenomenological Approach." *Reader-response Criticism: From Formalism to Poststructuralism*. Ed. Jane P. Tompkins. Baltimore: Johns Hopkins UP, 1980. Print.

İçöz, Nursel. "Domestic Violence in *The Black Prince*." *Hacettepe Üniversitesi Edebiyat Fakültesi Dergisi* 22:2, 2005, 41-59. Print.

Kennedy, Adrienne. "Funnyhouse of A Negro." *The Adrienne Kennedy Reader*. Ed. Werner Sollors. Minneapolis & London: U of Minnesota P, 2001. Print.

Knox, Bernard. Introduction. *The Theban Plays*. New York: Penguin, 1984. Print.

Kristeva, Julia. *Desire in Language: A Semiotic Approach to Literature and Art*. Ed. Leon S. Roudiez. Trans. Thomas Gora. New York: Columbia UP, 1980. Print.

Labute, Neil. *Medea Redux*. London: Faber and Faber, 2000. Print.

Leon-Portilla, Miguel. *Aztec Thought and Culture*. Trans. Jack Emory Davis. Norman: U of Oklahoma P, 2002. Print.

Levi-Strauss, Claude. *Myth and Meaning*. London: Routledge, 1978. Print.

Lochhead, Liz. *Bagpipe Muzak*. London: Penguin, 1991. Print.

--- . *Blood and Ice*. London: Nick Hern Books, 2009. Print.

--- . *Dreaming Frankenstein: and Collected Poems. Washington:* Meany P, 1985. Print.

--- . *Mary Queen of Scots Got Her Head Chopped Off, Dracula*. London and New York: Penguin, 1989. Print.

---. *Medea*. Guildford: Biddles, 2000. Print.

---. *Perfect Days*. London: Nick Hern Books, 1999. Print.

---. *Tartuffe*. Polygon P: 1986. Print.

---. *Thebans*. Surrey: Bookmarque, 2003. Print.

---. *True Confessions and New Cliches*. Edinburgh: Edinburgh UP, 1987. Print.

---. "An Interview with Liz Lochhead." Ed. Carla Rodriguez Gonzalez. ATLANTIS 26.1. 101-110 Print.

---. Interview. Ed. Emily B.Todd. *Verse* 8:3. 83-95. Print.

Lovato, Roberto. " 'Yo existo': The Woman of Color Breaks the Silence." *The City*. 1990: 23-24. Print.

Lyndsay, David. *Ane Satyre of the Thrie Estaitis*. London: Cassell P, 1954. Print.

Luschnig, C.A.E. "Medea In Corinth: Political Aspects of Euripides' *Medea*." *Digressus* 1 (2001). 8-28 Print.

MacKenzie, Donald A. *Scottish Wonder Tales From Myth and Legend*. Mineola, New York: Dover P, 1997. Print.

March, Cristie L. *Rewriting Scotland*. Manchester and New York: Manchester UP, 2002. Print.

Mayorga, Irma. 2001. "Homecoming: The Politics of Myth and Location in Cherrie L. Moraga's *The Hungry Woman: A Mexican Medea* and *Heart of the Earth:A Popul Vuh Story*." In Moraga 2001, 155-160. Print.

McDonald, Jan and Jeniffer Harvey. "Putting New Twists to Old Stories: Feminism and Lochhead's Drama." *Liz Lochhead's Voices*. Ed. Robert Crawford and Anne Varty. Edinburgh: Edinburgh UP, 1993. Print.

Merriam-Webster Dictionary. Springfield, Mass.: Merriam-Webster, 1997. Print.

Millett, Kate. *Sexual Politics*. London: Abacus, 1971. Print.

Milton, John. "Paradise Lost Book IV." *The Arnold Anthology of British and Irish Literature. Eds.* Robert Clark and Thomas Healey. London and Sydney: Arnold P, 1997. 397-415. Print.

Mitchell, Margaret. *Gone With The Wind.* New York: Macmillan, 1937. Print.

Moraga, Cherrie L, ed. *Cuentos: Stories By Latinas.* New York: Kitchen Table: Women of Color P, 1983. Print.

--- . *Heroes and Saints& Other Plays.* New Mexico: West End P, 2004. Print.

--- . *The Hungry Woman: A Mexican Medea and Heart of the Earth: A Popul Vuh Story.* New Mexico: West End P, 2003. Print.

--- . "Queer Aztlan: The Re-formation of Chicano Tribe.."*The Last Generation: Prose and Poetry.* Boston: South End P, 1993. Print.

--- . *Loving in the War Years.* Boston: South End P, 1983. Print.

Moraga, Cherrie and Gloria Anzaldua, eds. *This Bridge Called My Back: Writings by Radical Women of Color.* Berkeley: Third Woman P, 1984. Print.

Moraga,Cherrie . *Waiting in the Wings: Portrait of a Queer Motherhood.* Ithaca: Firebrand P, 1997. Print.

--- . *Watsonville, Circle In The Dirt.* New Mexico: West End P, 2002. Print.

--- . "A Challenge to Borderline from a Daughter of Aztlan: An Interview with Cherrie L. Moraga." Ed. İnci Bilgin. *JAST.* 'Special Chicana/o Issue'. Eds.Ayse Lahur Kirtunç and Maria Herrera Sobek V23. Spring 2006. Izmir: Ege UP. Print.

Morrison, Toni. *Beloved.* New York: Plume, 1988. Print.

Narayan, Uma and Sandra Harding (eds). *Decentering The Center: Philosophy For A Multicultural, Postcolonial and Feminist World.* Bloomington: Indiana UP, 2000. Print.

Nietzsche, Frederick. *The Geneology of Morals.* Trans. Horace Barnett Samuel. New York: Courier Dover P, 2003. Print.

---. "The Will To Power." *From Modernism to Postmodernism: an Anthology* Ed. Lawrence E. Cahoone. Oxford: Blackwell, 1996. Print.

Ramirez, Elizabeth C. *Chicanas/ Latinas in American Theatre: A History of Performance*. Bloomington and Indianapolis: Indiana UP, 2000. Print.

Redstocking. *Feminist Revolution*. New York: Random House, 1979. Print.

Rhys, Jean. *Wide Sargasso Sea*. Ed.Judith L.Raiskin. New York and London: Norton P, 1999. Print.

Rich, Adrienne. "Compulsory Heterosexuality and Lesbian Existence." *Powers of Desire: The Politics of Sexuality*. Eds. Ann Snitow, Christine Stansell, et al. New York: Monthly Review, 1993. Print.

---. *On Lies, Secrets, Silence*. London: Virago P, 1980. Print.

Said, Edward W. *Orientalism*. New York: Vintage, 1994. Print.

Salvidar-Hull, Sonia. Introduction. *The Borderlands*. San Fracisco: Aunt Lute Books, 1999. Print.

Sanchez, Elba Rosario. "Cartohistography: One's Voice's Continent." *Chicana Feminisms: A Critical Reader*. Eds. Gabriela F. Arredondo, et.al. Durham, NC: Duke UP, 2003. Print.

Sandoval-Sanchez, Alberto and Nancy Saporta Sternbach. *Stages of Life: Transcultural Performance Identity In U.S. Latina Theater*. Tucson: U of Arizona P, 2001. Print.

Scheler, Max. *Ressentiment*. Trans. Lewis B. Coser and William W. Holdheim. Milwaukee, WI: Marquette UP, 2003. Print.

Scott, Sir Walter. *Waverly*. London: Electronic Book Co., 2001. Print.

Selden, Raman and Peter Widdowson. *A Reader's Guide to Contemporary Literary Criticism*. Lexington: UP of Kentucky, 1993. Print.

Sellers, Susan. *Myth and Fairy Tale in Contemporary Women's Fiction*. Houndmills, Basingstoke, Hampshire; New York: Palgrave, 2001. Print.

Shakespeare, William. *Othello*. London and New York: Penguin, 2001. Print.

---. *Hamlet*. London: Edward Arnold, 1963. Print.

---. *The Taming of the Shrew*. Harmondsworth: Penguin, 1968. Print.

Showalter, Elaine. *A Literature of their Own: British Women Novelists from Bronte to Lessing*. London: Virago, 1999. Print.

Smith, Barbara. "Greece." *The Feminist Companion to Mythology*. Ed. Carolyne Larrington. London: Pandora, 1992. 65-101. Print.

---. "Racism and Women's Studies." *Frontiers: A Journal of Women's Studies* 5:1 (1980): [page numbers].

Smith, Ian Crichton. "The Beginning of a New Song." [More info needed. See MLA Handbook p. 181 ff.] www.edinburghliterarypubtour.co.uk/makars/smith/smith.pdf

Sollors, Werner. Introduction. *The Adrienne Kennedy Reader*. Minneapolis & London: U of Minnesota P, 2001. Print.

Sophocles. *Three Theban Plays*. New York and London: Penguin P, 1947. Print.

Spivak, Gayatri Chakravorty. "*Wide Sargasso Sea* and A Critique of Imperialism." *Wide Sargasso Sea*. Ed. Judith L. Raiskin. New York, London: Norton & Company P, 1999. Print.

---. *A Critique of Postcolonial Reason: Toward a History of the Vanishing Present*. Cambridge, Massachusetts, London: Harvard UP, 1999. Print.

---. *The Spivak Reader*. Eds. Landry and Gerald Maclean. New York and London: Routledge, 1996. Print.

---. *The post-colonial critic: interviews, strategies, dialogues*. Ed. Sarah Harasym. New York: Routledge, 1990. Print.

---. "Can the Subaltern Speak." *Colonial Discourse and Postcolonial Theory. A Reader*. Ed. Patrick Williams and Laura Chrisman. New York: Columbia UP, 1994. Print.

--- ."Bonding in Difference: An Interview with Spivak." Ed. Alfred Arteaga. *The Spivak Reader*. Ed. Donna Landry and Gerald MacLean. New York and London: Routledge, 1996. Print.

Stevenson, Robert Louis. *The Strange Case of Dr. Jekyll and Mr. Hyde*. Harmondsworth, Middlesex and New York: Penguin, 1994. Print.

--- . *Treasure Island*. Harmondsworth, Middlesex and New York: Penguin, 1994. Print.

Svich, Caridad. *Wreckage*. NoPassport, 2009. Print.

Tanrısal, Meldan. "Squaws and Princesses or Corn Maidens: Misconceptions and the Truths about Native American Women." The second Cultural Studies Seminar, *Proceedings of The History of Culture, the Culture of History*. İzmir: Ege U, 1997. Print.

Tedlock, Dennis, trans. *Popol Vuh: the Definitive Edition of the Mayan Book of the Dawn of Life and the Glories of Gods and Kings*. New York: Simon and Schuster, 1985. Print.

--- . *Rabinal Achi. A Mayan Drama of War and Sacrifice*. Oxford: Oxford UP, 2003. Print.

Tejumola, Olaniyan. *Scars of conquest/masks of resistance: the invention of cultural identities in African, African-American, and Caribbean drama*. New York: Oxford UP, 1995. Print.

Thomas, Julia (ed). *Reading Images*. New York: Palgrave, 2001. Print.

Underiner, Tamara L. *Contemporary Theatre in Mayan Mexico*. Austin: U of Texas P, 2004. Print.

Valdez, Luis. *Zoot Suit and Other Plays*. Houston, TX: Arte Publico P, 1992. Print.

Walker, Alice. *The Color Purple*. New York and London: Pocket Books, 1985. Print.

Weedon, Chris. *Feminist Practice & Poststructuralist Theory*. Oxford: Blackwell, 1997. Print.

Whyte, Christopher. (ed). *Gendering The Nation: Studies in Modern Scottish Literature*. Edinburgh: Edinburgh UP, 1995. Print.

Wolf, Naomi. "The Beauty Myth." *Women in Culture: A Women's Studies Anthology*. Ed. Lucinda Joy Peach. Massachussetts, Oxford: Blackwell, 1998. Print.

Wolf, Christa. *Medea*: *A Modern Retelling*. Trans. John Cullen. New York: Nan A. Talese, 2005. Print.

Woolf, Virginia. *Mrs. Dalloway*. London: Penguin, 1996. Print.

----. *A Room of One's Own*. New York: Harcourt, Brace and Co., 1929. Print.

Young, Robert. *White Mythologies*: *Writing History and The West*. London: Routledge, 1990. Print.

ibidem-Verlag
Melchiorstr. 15
D-70439 Stuttgart
info@ibidem-verlag.de

www.ibidem-verlag.de
www.ibidem.eu
www.edition-noema.de
www.autorenbetreuung.de